OECD Development Co-operation Peer Reviews: Ireland 2020

This work is published under the responsibility of the Secretary-General of the OECD. The opinions expressed and arguments employed herein do not necessarily reflect the official views of OECD member countries.

This document, as well as any data and map included herein, are without prejudice to the status of or sovereignty over any territory, to the delimitation of international frontiers and boundaries and to the name of any territory, city or area.

Please cite this publication as:
OECD (2020), *OECD Development Co-operation Peer Reviews: Ireland 2020*, OECD Development Co-operation Peer Reviews, OECD Publishing, Paris, *https://doi.org/10.1787/c20f6995-en*.

ISBN 978-92-64-92783-4 (print)
ISBN 978-92-64-66394-7 (pdf)

OECD Development Co-operation Peer Reviews
ISSN 2309-7124 (print)
ISSN 2309-7132 (online)

Foreword

The OECD Development Assistance Committee (DAC) conducts periodic reviews of the individual development co-operation efforts of DAC members. The policies and programmes of each member are critically examined approximately once every five to six years, with five members reviewed annually.

The objectives of DAC peer reviews are to improve the quality and effectiveness of development co-operation policies and systems, and to promote good development partnerships for greater impact on poverty reduction and sustainable development in developing countries. DAC peer reviews assess the performance of a given member and examine both policy and implementation. They take an integrated, system-wide perspective on the development co-operation and humanitarian assistance activities of the member under review.

The OECD Development Co-operation Directorate provides analytical support to each review and is responsible for developing and maintaining, in close consultation with the Committee, the methodology and analytical framework – known as the Reference Guide – within which the peer reviews are undertaken.

Following the submission of a memorandum by the reviewed member, setting out key policy and programme developments, the Secretariat and two DAC members designated as peer reviewers visit the member's capital to interview officials, parliamentarians, as well as civil society and non-governmental organisations' representatives. This is followed by a field visit, where the team meet with senior officials and representatives of the partner country or territory's administration, parliamentarians, civil society and other development partners. The main findings of these consultations and a set of recommendations are then discussed during a formal meeting of the DAC prior to finalisation of the report.

The Peer Review of Ireland involved an extensive process of consultation with actors and stakeholders in Dublin and Limerick, Ireland and Addis Ababa, Ethiopia, in September and October 2019. The resulting report, which contains both the main findings and recommendations of the DAC and the analytical report of the Secretariat, was approved on 2 April 2020.

The peer review took into account the political and economic context in Ireland, to the extent that it shapes Ireland's development co-operation policies and systems. However, the drafting of the peer review including its main findings and recommendations preceded the COVID-19 pandemic.

Taoiseach (Prime Minister) Leo Varadkar of the Fine Gael party took office in 2017. The minority government of Fine Gael and independent members had been underpinned by a "confidence and supply" arrangement with the main opposition party, Fianna Fáil. General elections took place in February 2020 and a new government is in the process of being formed.

Ireland is emerging from what is dubbed "a lost decade". The global financial crisis that started in 2008 threatened the stability of private banks as well as public finance in Ireland and increased unemployment. Ireland required a bailout and support from the International Monetary Fund, the European Central Bank and the European Commission. Painful reform measures spurred Ireland's recovery, with renewed high growth since 2013. In 2015, Ireland's gross national income (GNI) per capita surpassed its 2007 levels. Ireland has already repaid large parts of the bailout. Unemployment dropped from 11.9% in 2014 to 5.8% in 2018 and is projected to further decrease.

Internal challenges persist. Ireland's population is growing at a rate of 1.1% in 2017, far above other European Union (EU) countries. This is putting pressure on the job market, housing and infrastructure, against a backdrop of reduced investment during the economic crisis, and is increasing demands on the health sector. The planned transformation towards decarbonising the economy is making only slow progress, and Ireland is projected to miss its 2020 climate change emission targets.

Brexit and other external factors create uncertainty. The United Kingdom is one of Ireland's most important trading partners and the establishment of an EU external border between them is expected to slow growth. Ireland anticipates it may need to introduce a budget deficit, although debt is still high (the Central Statistics Office calculates debt at 104% using its modified gross national income measure). The 1998 Good Friday peace agreement put an end to decades of violence, aided by the softening of the land border between Ireland and Northern Ireland, but there is fear that Brexit could reignite tension in Northern Ireland. Ireland could also be affected by global agreements on corporate taxation, while pressure on the multilateral trade system increase risks for Ireland's open economy.

To sustain economic growth, Ireland is set to rely on and diversify its open economy. In the foreword to the foreign policy document, Global Ireland, Taoiseach Varadkar said, "We are at a moment in world history where we can turn inwards and become irrelevant, or we can open ourselves to opportunities and possibilities on a global scale that we have never had before". Ireland aims to substantially diversify its trade relations and partnerships with countries around the world, with the ambition to double its global footprint by 2025. Opening new diplomatic missions, active outreach across the globe and Ireland's campaign for a non-permanent seat on the United Nations Security Council are part of these efforts.

The set-up of Ireland's development co-operation system has been stable. Ireland has steadily pushed forward integration of development co-operation in the Department of Foreign Affairs and Trade (DFAT). The Development Co-operation and Africa Division within the department steers and co-ordinates policies of Irish development co-operation and manages the bulk of Irish official development assistance (ODA).

The effects of the financial crisis affected DFAT still in the period under review. The public sector was heavily impacted by the crisis, which led to reductions in overall spending and staffing, and pay cuts. The previous peer review in 2014 acknowledged these challenges and found that Ireland had managed to continue its co-operation and implement budget cuts with as few negative effects for partners as possible. Since the last peer review, Ireland has steadily increased ODA volumes but not yet reached pre-crisis levels. And only towards the end of the period under review could DFAT start remedying staffing cuts and rebuilding its capacity.

Ireland now anticipates expanding its activities. In February 2019, Ireland launched its new international development policy, A Better World, after an extensive consultation process. In the spirit of the 2030 Agenda for Sustainable Development, Ireland affirms its strong commitment to reaching the poorest and most vulnerable by making the furthest behind first the guiding principle of its development co-operation.

A 2018 review by the Joint Committee on Foreign Affairs and Trade, and Defence of both parliamentary chambers expressed strong support for Irish development co-operation. The committee made numerous recommendations, including to attain the level of 0.7% of GNI as ODA, take action on policy coherence for sustainable development, and maintain a focus on least developed and fragile countries and on the poorest and most vulnerable segments of populations.

Acknowledgments

Development Assistance Committee (DAC) peer reviews function as a tool for both learning and accountability. This report – containing both the main findings and recommendations of the DAC and the analytical report of the Secretariat – is the result of a 9-month in-depth consultation and review process. It was produced by a review team comprising peer reviewers from Australia (Cate Rogers, Department of Foreign Affairs and Trade, and Rebecca Shaw, Department of Foreign Affairs and Trade) and Slovenia (Uroš Vajgl, Ministry of Foreign Affairs). From the OECD Development Co-operation Directorate, Santhosh Persaud, Policy Analyst, served as the lead analyst for the review, together with Thomas Boehler, Policy Analyst, Claudio Cerabino, Junior Policy Analyst, Karin McDonald, Policy Analyst, and Rachel Scott, Senior Policy Analyst. Katia Grosheva provided logistical assistance to the review, and formatted and produced the report. The report was prepared under the supervision of Rahul Malhotra, Head of Division, Reviews, Results, Evaluation and Development Innovation. The report was edited by Susan Sachs.

The team are grateful for valuable inputs from across the Development Co-operation Directorate, including statistical support from the Financing for Sustainable Development division, and OECD, in particular the OECD Economics Department, the Directorate for Financial and Enterprise Affairs, the Centre for Tax Policy and Administration, the Directorate for Public Governance, the Directorate for Employment, Labour and Social Affairs, the Environment Directorate, the Trade and Agriculture Directorate and the Development Centre. The team also valued inputs from the Multilateral Organisation Performance Assessment Network.

The Peer Review of Ireland benefited throughout the process from the commitment and dedication of representatives of the Irish Department of Foreign Affairs and Trade. The review team are also thankful to the team of the Irish Embassy in Ethiopia, who ensured smooth contact with local counterparts as well as logistical support.

Table of contents

FIGURES

INFOGRAPHICS

TABLES

Follow OECD Publications on:

http://twitter.com/OECD_Pubs

http://www.facebook.com/OECDPublications

http://www.linkedin.com/groups/OECD-Publications-4645871

http://www.youtube.com/oecdilibrary

http://www.oecd.org/oecddirect/

This book has...

StatLinks ᴀᴵˢᴸ

A service that delivers Excel® files from the printed page!

Look for the *StatLinks* ᴀᴵˢᴸ at the bottom of the tables or graphs in this book. To download the matching Excel® spreadsheet, just type the link into your Internet browser, starting with the *https://doi.org* prefix, or click on the link from the e-book edition.

Abbreviations and acronyms

AADP	Africa Agri-Food Development Programme
BEPS	Base erosion and profit shifting
CRS	Creditor Reporting System
CSO	Civil society organisation
DAC	Development Assistance Committee
DCAD	Development Cooperation and Africa Division
DES	Department of Education and Skills
DFAT	Department of Foreign Affairs and Trade
DRM	Domestic resource mobilisation
EAU	Evaluation and Audit Unit
EU	European Union
FDI	Foreign direct investment
GNI	Gross national income
GPEDC	Global Partnership for Effective Development Co-operation
HQ	Headquarters
IATI	International Aid Transparency Initiative
ICRC	International Committee of the Red Cross
IDC	Inter-departmental committee
IT	Information technology
LDC	Least developed country
MDB	Multilateral development bank
NGO	Non-governmental organisation
ODA	Official development assistance
OECD	Organisation for Economic Co-operation and Development
PCSD	Policy coherence for sustainable development
PSE	Private sector engagement
PSEAH	Preventing Sexual Exploitation, Abuse and Harassment
SAGM	Standard Approach to Grant Management
SDG	Sustainable Development Goal

SIDS	Small island developing states
UN	United Nations
UNCTAD	United Nations Conference on Trade and Development
UNDP	United Nations Development Programme
UNHCR	United Nations High Commissioner for Refugees

Signs used:

EUR	Euro
USD	United States dollar
( )	Secretariat estimate in whole or part
	(Nil)
0.0	Negligible
..	Not available
...	Not available separately but included in total
n.a.	Not applicable
p	Provisional

Slight discrepancies in totals are due to rounding.

Annual average exchange rate: 1 USD = EUR

2011	2012	2013	2014	2015	2016	2017	2018
0.7192	0.7780	0.7532	0.7537	0.9015	0.9043	0.8871	0.8473

Executive summary

Ireland has been a member of the Development Assistance Committee (DAC) since 1985 and was last reviewed in 2014. This report reviews progress since then, highlights recent successes and challenges, and provides key recommendations for going forward. Ireland has partially implemented 71% of the recommendations made in 2014, and fully implemented 29%.

This review – containing both the main findings and recommendations of the DAC and the analytical report of the Secretariat – was prepared with reviewers from Australia and Slovenia for the DAC Peer Review of Ireland and adopted at the OECD on 2 April 2020. In conducting the review, the team consulted key institutions and partners in Dublin and Limerick, Ireland and in the field in Addis Ababa, Ethiopia in September and October 2019. The drafting of the peer review including its main findings and recommendations preceded the COVID-19 pandemic.

Global development efforts. Ireland shows leadership in global policy debates and national development education and can build on its progress in making its policies coherent with sustainable development abroad. As a successful influencer of global policies, Ireland has co-facilitated the adoption of important global frameworks and advocates effectively on priorities such as women, peace and security. Ireland is making serious efforts to address policy coherence issues such as taxation and health worker migration, while domestic action against climate change remains an important challenge. Ireland should move towards more systematically addressing coherence challenges. Ireland has a strong approach to development education. Further investments could help to deepen and sustain the very solid support within the Irish population. Ireland's new narrative on international development is an opportunity to strengthen its communications.

Policy vision and framework. Ireland has put forward an engaging new vision for its development co-operation, and now needs to update its policy framework and operational guidance. Building on broad consultations, the 2019 policy for international development, *A Better World*, sets as Ireland's prime ambition reaching the furthest behind first, prioritising such issues as gender equality and humanitarian need. Ireland focuses on least developed and fragile contexts as well as sectors that correspond to its strengths. It plans to update and develop operational guidance, which will be critically important for the implementation of *A Better World* by staff and partners. Driven by the ambition to expand its global footprint, Ireland needs to manage the risk of not spreading itself too thin. Ireland's approach to partnerships reflects the strong support for civil society and dedication to multilateralism that are hallmarks of its development co-operation. Ireland considers its membership of the European Union (EU) as essential to its relations with the rest of the world, and intends to contribute even more actively to shaping European external engagement. Despite an expansion of activities, Ireland still needs to clearly articulate a strategic approach for its private sector engagement that builds on its niche in the agri-food sector.

Financing for development. Ireland focuses ODA on its priorities, such as least developed countries, but it needs to increase overall financing to meet its ambition and commitment. Ireland has a strong political commitment to reach 0.7% of gross national income (GNI) as ODA, but growth in ODA volume has not translated into progress towards this target during the recovery from the impact of the 2008 financial crisis. Ireland therefore requires a clear plan for when and how to increase spending and to invest in necessary capacities. Bilateral ODA focuses on Ireland's geographic and thematic priorities, almost meeting the commitment of allocating 0.15% of GNI to least developed countries. Multilateral ODA is of high quality, with significant voluntary core funding and the use of multi-donor pooled funds. Growing the ODA budget is an opportunity for Ireland to increase its financial weight in priority countries and organisations in line with its policy influence. While Ireland's financial instruments to mobilise private finance are still limited, it advocates for improving the development relevance of private finance, including with the EU, and has launched a whole of government approach for domestic revenue mobilisation in partner countries.

Structure and systems. Ireland has clear structures and systems in place but needs to address human resources challenges and anticipate needs from a growing budget. The Department of Foreign Affairs and Trade (DFAT) leads Irish development co-operation. Ireland wants to further improve collaboration across government, building on existing good practices. A Standard Approach to Grant Management has clarified decision-making. Risk management processes are clear and controls effective. Ireland is also taking steps to respond to the new DAC recommendation on preventing sexual exploitation and abuse. Growth in the ODA budget will require further reflection on co-ordination, which partially relies on informal contacts at present, and on effective quality assurance as well as investment in information technology and e-based processes. Implementation of the DFAT human resources strategic action plan is an opportunity to address important human resources challenges. Low levels of staffing and high levels of turnover affect the level and quality of engagement. Ireland also needs to clarify how it wants to match skills and jobs and mobilise expertise for the priorities of *A Better World.*

Delivery and partnerships. Quality partnerships with civil society and multilaterals are essential drivers of Ireland's development co-operation, while its strong engagement at country level could benefit from some adjustments. Ireland's partnerships with civil society are particularly strong and characterised by quality funding and regular, open dialogue. Ireland is also much appreciated for its constructive engagement in multilateral organisations. Building on good funding practices, including multi-year allocations, Ireland seeks to intensify strategic dialogue with its multilateral partners. Ireland also wants to strengthen research partnerships and intensify dialogue with private sector actors. At country level, Ireland takes a proactive role in donor co-ordination and political dialogue. It uses joint approaches and continues to champion development effectiveness. Informed by 2018 data on development effectiveness, Ireland could promote ownership, alignment, the use of country systems and medium-term predictability to further improve.

Results, evaluation and learning. Ireland is strongly committed to results-based management and evaluation and would benefit from investments in knowledge management. Ireland uses results information to adapt programme design and implementation and is now planning to develop a new results-based management approach to inform strategic decision making and learning. The independent Evaluation and Audit Unit identifies strategic evaluation topics, disseminates evaluation findings and tracks the implementation of recommendations. A recent staff increase and a new evaluation policy will allow it to expand its engagement. However, learning often stays within the team that generated it. Building on its own good practices, Ireland could further invest in knowledge management, in particular as the ODA budget grows.

Fragility, crises and humanitarian aid. Ireland is an excellent humanitarian partner and has a unique approach to fragility. *A Better World* has a strong focus on fragility and reducing humanitarian need, in line with the push by Ireland to reach the furthest behind first. Allocations follow intentions, with a large share of ODA going to fragile contexts. A good range of tools – diplomatic, development and humanitarian – ensure that Ireland, also drawing on its own history, can design an appropriate response to individual fragile contexts. Its very flexible funding models, especially for humanitarian assistance, could provide useful inspiration for other DAC donors. There are good efforts to align internal funding streams to support the humanitarian-development-peace nexus. The model for Ireland's humanitarian programme is built on its influencing power and Ireland will need to take care that it invests in the needed staffing capacities.

The DAC's recommendations to Ireland

1. Ireland should further develop mechanisms for analysing the impact of its domestic policies on developing countries, identify potential inconsistencies, discuss action to address these with all stakeholders, and ensure that progress is monitored.

2. Ireland should further improve the alignment to and use of country-owned results frameworks as well as its medium-term predictability and transparency in government-to-government partnerships.

3. Ireland should finalise a private sector engagement strategy that builds on its niche and focuses on development impact, in particular for the benefit of marginalised populations.

4. Ireland should assess its quality assurance mechanisms to ensure priorities, evidence, and cross-cutting and safeguarding issues are adequately reflected across all grant management phases.

5. Ireland should invest in knowledge management and, in particular:

   a. systematically capture and disseminate lessons from programming and findings of all evaluations

   b. expand knowledge sharing mechanisms to strengthen thematic expertise.

6. Ireland should develop operational guidance on both reaching the furthest behind first and its top priorities, and it should implement a plan to roll out this guidance to staff and partners.

7. Ireland should advance its approach to results-based management by:

   a. promoting a results and learning culture, and strengthening capacities to manage for results across the system

   b. adopting results frameworks that spell out the expected results chain, using SDG targets and indicators, and enable a clear focus on those furthest behind.

8. To increase its ODA budget and meet its international commitment of 0.7% of GNI by 2030, Ireland should develop and implement a comprehensive plan that identifies how to grow spending, and communicate the value of international development to the parliament and public.

9. Ireland should undertake strategic workforce planning to ensure it has the appropriate skills, expertise and capabilities to deliver on its expanding development co-operation objectives.

Figure 0.1. Ireland's aid at a glance

Net ODA	2017	2018	Change 2017/18	ODA grant equivalent 2018
Current (USD m)	838	934	11.5%	934
Constant (2017 USD m)	838	891	6.3%	891
In Euro (million)	743	792	6.5%	792
ODA/GNI	0.32%			0.31%
Bilateral share	59%	57%		57%

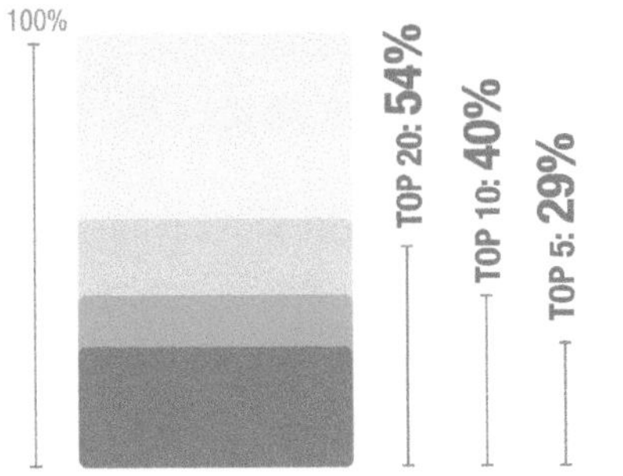

HOW CONCENTRATED IS IRELAND'S ODA?
Share of ODA to top recipients, gross bilateral ODA

TOP 20: 54% TOP 10: 40% TOP 5: 29%

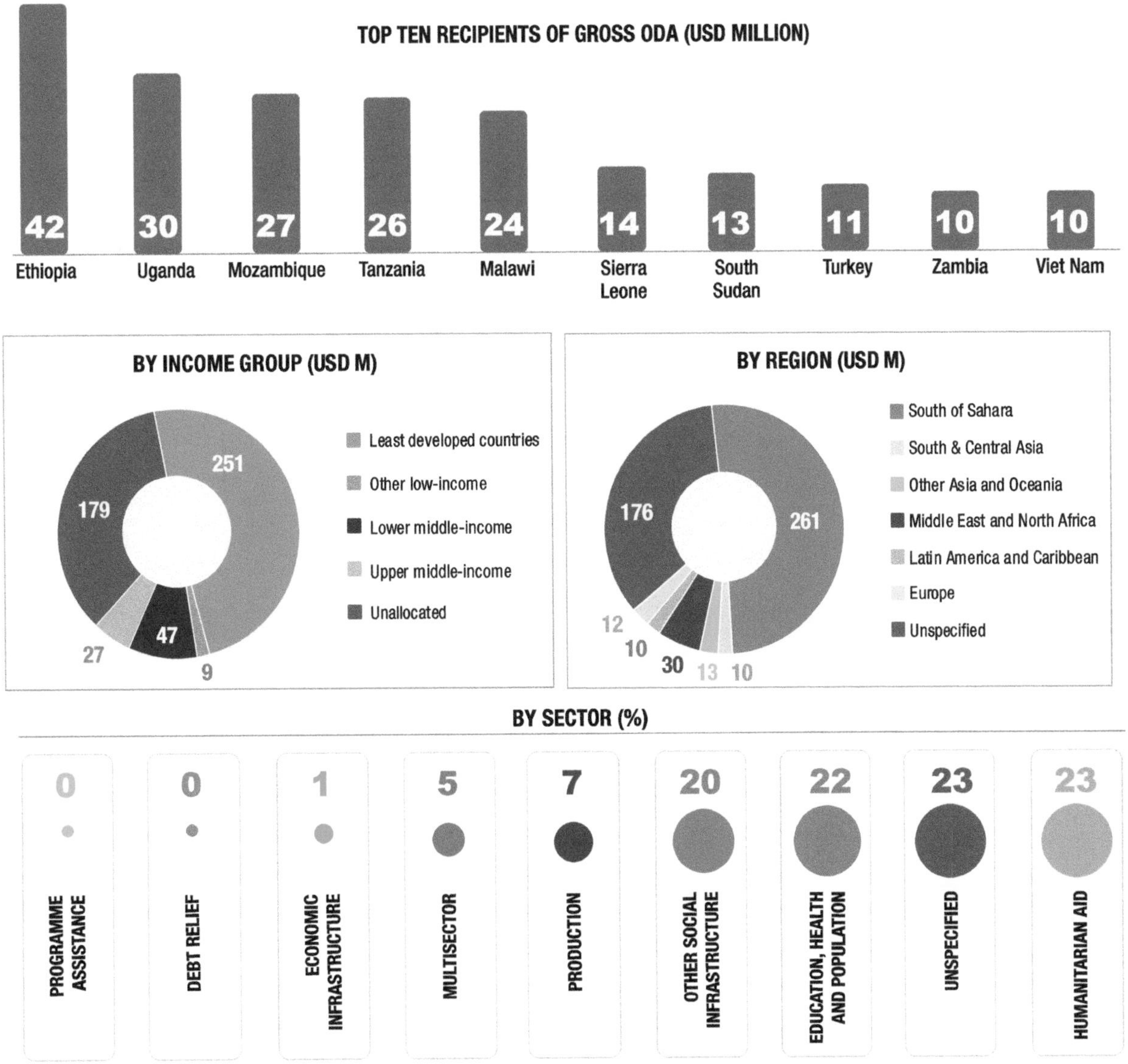

TOP TEN RECIPIENTS OF GROSS ODA (USD MILLION)

Ethiopia	Uganda	Mozambique	Tanzania	Malawi	Sierra Leone	South Sudan	Turkey	Zambia	Viet Nam
42	30	27	26	24	14	13	11	10	10

BY INCOME GROUP (USD M)

251, 179, 27, 9, 47

- Least developed countries
- Other low-income
- Lower middle-income
- Upper middle-income
- Unallocated

BY REGION (USD M)

261, 176, 12, 10, 30, 13, 10

- South of Sahara
- South & Central Asia
- Other Asia and Oceania
- Middle East and North Africa
- Latin America and Caribbean
- Europe
- Unspecified

BY SECTOR (%)

PROGRAMME ASSISTANCE	DEBT RELIEF	ECONOMIC INFRASTRUCTURE	MULTISECTOR	PRODUCTION	OTHER SOCIAL INFRASTRUCTURE	EDUCATION, HEALTH AND POPULATION	UNSPECIFIED	HUMANITARIAN AID
0	0	1	5	7	20	22	23	23

Gross bilateral ODA, 2017-18 average, unless otherwise shown

Source: (OECD, 2019[1]), *Creditor Reporting System* (database), https://stats.oecd.org/Index.aspx?DataSetCode=crs1.

StatLink https://doi.org/10.1787/888934121107

Infographic 1. Findings from the 2020 Development Co-operation Peer Review of Ireland

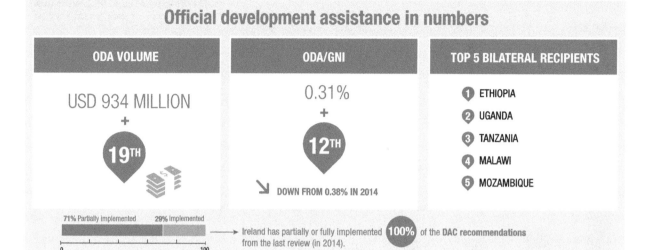

Official development assistance in numbers

ODA VOLUME	ODA/GNI	TOP 5 BILATERAL RECIPIENTS
USD 934 MILLION + 19TH	0.31% + 12TH DOWN FROM 0.38% IN 2014	1 ETHIOPIA 2 UGANDA 3 TANZANIA 4 MALAWI 5 MOZAMBIQUE

71% Partially implemented 29% Implemented

0   100

→ Ireland has partially or fully implemented **100%** of the DAC recommendations from the last review (in 2014).

As a valued development partner, Ireland...

...is a **strong voice** for sustainable development.

Leading and supporting policy dialogue at international and country levels.

...invests in **quality partnerships** with civil society.

Characterised by mutual trust, and flexible and reliable funding.

...has a **strong approach to fragility.**

Combining development support, diplomacy and excellent humanitarian donorship.

Ireland can improve by...

...**increasing ODA** in line with its policy *A Better World.*

...**ensuring staff capacity** and skills to deliver on its priorities.

... **developing guidance and results frameworks** to help staff and partners reach the furthest behind first.

Figures based on 2018 data, the most recent complete data reported by DAC members to the OECD Creditor Reporting System (CRS), and in current prices. ODA volume and ODA/GNI rankings are among DAC countries. Top 5 recipients are of bilateral ODA in 2018.

The DAC's main findings and recommendations

Ireland is a strong development partner

A new ambition

Irish development co-operation has pulled through a tough decade. Following the global financial crisis and recession in Ireland, Irish development co-operation had to weather cuts in staffing, pay and spending. Ireland's economy is now back on track and official development assistance (ODA) started growing again in 2015. Today, Irish development co-operation is strong, and with many areas of excellence.

Driven by a new ambition, Ireland has decided to do more and do better. In the 2018 policy document Global Ireland, the government calls for doubling Ireland's global footprint by 2025. Ireland is opening new diplomatic missions, competing for a seat on the United Nations Security Council, exploring new trade partnerships, deepening and expanding engagement with Africa, and building up relations with Asia, the Middle East, Latin America and small island developing states. Development co-operation is integral to this new ambition.

Ireland's prime ambition is reaching the furthest behind first. This is the overarching goal of A Better World, Ireland's 2019 policy for international development. For Ireland, development co-operation is about both values and self-interest: it helps alleviate poverty, vulnerability and inequality, brings shared prosperity, sustains friendships, enhances global influence and opens markets. A Better World focuses on Irish strengths such as reducing humanitarian need, strengthening governance, and promoting gender equality. Climate action is also a top priority. To reach its objectives, Ireland foresees a significant increase in its ODA budget in line with its international commitments. Broad consultations on A Better World have shown that Ireland's population, development community and politicians all strongly support the new vision and ambition for Irish development co-operation.

Sustaining Ireland's strengths will help to deliver the new ambition

Ireland is a strong voice for sustainable development, leading and supporting policy dialogue at both international and local levels. It has facilitated the adoption of key global frameworks, notably the 2030 Agenda and the New York Declaration for Refugees and Migrants, and is successfully influencing global debates on its priorities such as women, peace and security. In partner countries, Ireland takes lead roles in political dialogue and donor co-ordination, including on challenging topics.

Walking the talk, Ireland allocates its ODA to least developed countries (75% of its country allocable aid in 2017) and fragile states, priority partners and sectors. Ireland provides only grants, which are almost 100% untied. This clear focus enables Ireland, as a relatively small donor, to exercise leadership and make a visible difference. Ireland is now adding regional approaches to its portfolio and aims to expand its engagement in both volume and scope.

Ireland is a leading advocate for multilateralism and civic space, and is engaging in close dialogue with its partner organisations, including at country level. As a result, civil society partnerships are characterised by mutual trust and flexible and reliable funding. Ireland is appreciated for its constructive engagement on the boards and governance bodies of multilateral organisations, where it advocates for poverty reduction and responses to partner countries' needs. Ireland provides significant core funding and extends multi-annual allocations to a number of its multilateral partners. Ireland considers its membership of the European Union (EU) essential to its relations with the rest of the world, and it intends to contribute even more actively to shaping European external engagement.

Ireland is an excellent humanitarian partner and has a unique approach to fragility. A good range of tools – diplomatic, development and humanitarian – ensure that Ireland can design an appropriate response to individual fragile contexts, based on its own history. Ireland's flexible funding models, especially for humanitarian assistance, could provide useful inspiration for other DAC donors. There are good efforts to align internal funding streams to support the humanitarian-development-peace nexus.

Ireland has a strong approach to development education which focuses on achieving greater knowledge and changed attitudes. Its approach encompasses both formal and non-formal education and relies on strong partnerships among the government, non-governmental organisations, education actors and local communities. Outreach to schools is already very substantial, and Ireland is aiming to reach wider audiences to sustain and deepen the considerable support within the Irish population.

Ireland can build on its achievements

Working across government, in particular to enhance policy coherence for sustainable development

Ireland is stepping up collaboration on development programming across government departments. The Department of Foreign Affairs and Trade (DFAT) is the clear lead for Ireland's international co-operation. There are already numerous good examples of collaboration between DFAT and other line departments including joint initiatives and staff exchanges. A revamped inter-departmental committee will provide opportunities for strategic exchange. It will also allow departments to share technical expertise and to benefit from DFAT's advice on quality co-operation.

Ireland is making progress on policy coherence for sustainable development in developing countries, but more work is required. It has undertaken a spillover analysis and has improved tax policies, engages on health worker migration and consistently sends troops to United Nations peacekeeping operations. Ireland has a strong focus on climate change adaptation in its development co-operation. However, in line with the ambition set forth in *A Better World* to be a "good citizen of the world", it also needs to progress in its domestic response to climate change. With the 2019 Climate Action Plan, the government has taken an important step in this direction. As pointed out in the last peer review, Ireland also needs to improve the mechanisms it uses to identify potential areas of incoherence between its domestic policies and development objectives and to systematically assess and monitor progress in addressing these.

Recommendation

1. Ireland should further develop mechanisms for analysing the impact of its domestic policies on developing countries, identify potential inconsistencies, discuss action to address these with all stakeholders, and ensure that progress is monitored.

Building on a strong foundation to enhance the effectiveness of partnerships

Ireland's partnership approach is one of its trademarks, but it has scope to make its partnerships even more effective. When updating the strategies for multilateral, civil society and research partnerships and finalising its private sector strategy, Ireland could focus on articulating how each contributes to Ireland's objectives, in particular in the more challenging environments where Ireland operates. Clarifying the added value of different types of partners would help Ireland to decide how to best scale up its ODA budget so as to ensure sustainable results and not overstretch its capacities and systems. Ireland could also explore how to facilitate collaboration among its partners, building on existing dialogue platforms that bring together various Irish stakeholders.

Ireland is an active, respected player in its partner countries, and aims to work with and through partner country governments where possible, despite often challenging contexts. It continues to take a proactive role in joint approaches, donor co-ordination and political dialogue, and takes country context as the starting point for its strategic planning and programming. Building on its close relationships with partner country governments and other actors in-country, Ireland should further strengthen country ownership and leadership by making greater use of country results frameworks and fully aligning its mission strategies to country priorities, as highlighted by 2018 data on development effectiveness. It should also publish data on its projects and performance-related information more regularly and make available forward-looking expenditure plans.

Ireland still lacks a clearly articulated approach to private sector engagement, although it has stepped up its activities since the last peer review, including engaging with the EU on responsible private sector investment for sustainable development. A private sector strategy, currently being prepared, will help Ireland to sharpen its niche in a competitive donor environment by building on its experiences to date, especially in the agri-food sector. The strategy should have a clear focus on the development impact of Ireland's private sector engagement on marginalised populations, which falls squarely within Ireland's overall priorities. Such a focus would also require articulating the government's risk appetite for investing in private sector partnerships.

Recommendations

2. Ireland should further improve the alignment to and use of country-owned results frameworks as well as its medium-term predictability and transparency in government-to-government partnerships.
3. Ireland should finalise a private sector engagement strategy that builds on its niche and focuses on development impact, in particular for the benefit of marginalised populations.

Readying systems and knowledge management to support the more ambitious development programme

Most Irish development co-operation systems function well, but Ireland needs to build them up to deliver a larger and more complex ODA portfolio. Ireland has invested in greater standardisation of its grant management and significantly improved its risk management. It is developing a specific policy on preventing sexual exploitation, abuse and harassment in line with the 2019 DAC recommendation. Building on its solid risk management, Ireland could complete its guidance on safeguarding issues and continue to build on anti-corruption efforts beyond the management of its grants. DFAT has also recognised the need for more e-based processes and investment in information technology infrastructure. In a growing system, these would help to maintain efficiency and also facilitate co-ordination, which relies in many ways on informal contacts. Moving forward, Ireland should also clarify where it sees the right balance on quality assurance to avoid overreliance on either grant managers or technical experts. The planned management review will help Ireland to assess the need for adjustments in its systems.

Ireland has a strong focus on learning. Self-reflection, broad consultation and evaluations inform strategic decision making. Operating mostly in challenging contexts, Ireland is willing to take risks, and it gives space for innovation, monitors results and takes adaptive action. Recent, much-needed investments in the capacity of the DFAT Evaluation and Audit Unit will help it to disseminate findings and enhance its support to other units in their conduct of evaluations. However, knowledge management on development co-operation is not systematic, despite a recommendation in Ireland's 2014 peer review. At present, sharing lessons beyond the team in question often relies on informal contacts between staff, with a high risk of losing knowledge. Nevertheless, Ireland has good practices to build on such as regional thematic workshops and communities of practice.

Recommendations

4. Ireland should assess its quality assurance mechanisms to ensure priorities, evidence, and cross-cutting and safeguarding issues are adequately reflected across all grant management phases.

5. Ireland should invest in knowledge management and, in particular:
   a. systematically capture and disseminate lessons from programming and findings of all evaluations
   b. expand knowledge sharing mechanisms to strengthen thematic expertise.

To deliver on its vision, Ireland will need to address some challenges

Translating the ambition of A Better World into operations

With *A Better World*, Ireland has created an ambitious – and still relatively new – vision that inspires staff, partners and the public. Ireland is already planning operational guidance to translate into practice the new policy priorities and ways of working outlined in *A Better World*. Staff and partners need clear and accessible guidelines to adapt targeting, intervention logic, ambition and risk appetite to reach the furthest behind first, the overarching goal of the new development policy. Moreover, Ireland aims to develop or update guidance on its top policy priorities. This should articulate the interlinkages between priorities and with intervention areas. To ensure guidance is applied in practice, staff and partners will also require training, support and systemic incentives.

Building on its strong commitment to results, Ireland also needs to define its new approach to managing for the sustainable development results that it aims to achieve. Ireland is setting up an Accountability Framework to track the implementation of top-level commitments and has plans to establish a more comprehensive results management approach in order to inform strategic decision-making, learning and adaptation. Aligning with the SDGs and partner countries can help to make a future results framework more useful and manageable for both Ireland and partners. Moreover, although monitoring at programme level has significantly improved, capacity and skills vary across the system.

Recommendations

6. Ireland should develop operational guidance on both reaching the furthest behind first and its top priorities, and it should implement a plan to roll out this guidance to staff and partners.
7. Ireland should advance its approach to results-based management by:
   a. promoting a results and learning culture, and strengthening capacities to manage for results across the system
   b. adopting results frameworks that spell out the expected results chain, using SDG targets and indicators, and enable a clear focus on those furthest behind.

Mobilising and managing a significantly higher ODA budget

Over the years, Ireland has maintained a strong commitment to providing 0.7% of its gross national income (GNI) as ODA and, as was noted in the 2014 peer review, both the public and political parties support a rise in the budget. Following the severe economic contraction in Ireland (2009-2014), this ambition has not been realised. Since 2015, while the ODA budget has grown, the ODA-to-GNI ratio has remained at around 0.31%. This contrasts with Ireland's undertaking to move towards the 0.7% target when its economy improves.

Significantly increasing the ODA budget requires a solid plan. Ireland benefits from strong economic growth that is projected to continue at 3% over the coming years. Based on these projections, meeting the 0.7% commitment would require Ireland to triple its current ODA budget by 2030. Managing such an increase would also require identifying the best-suited delivery channels, scaling up capacity for grant management, reflecting economic uncertainty and continuously making the case to the public.

Recommendation

8. To increase its ODA budget and meet its international commitment of 0.7% of GNI by 2030, Ireland should develop and implement a comprehensive plan that identifies how to grow spending, and communicate the value of international development to the parliament and public.

Investing in necessary human resources

Human resources are essential for Ireland to get the most out of its global profile and expanded development portfolio, as noted in Ireland's 2014 peer review. Ireland's development co-operation model strongly relies on its dedicated staff, in that they ensure close and regular engagement with partners and fill leadership roles at global and local level that give Ireland its influencing power. Ireland is taking action to reverse significant staffing cuts, but it will need to ensure it has sufficient capabilities to deliver on its priorities and notably assess how a growing budget will affect staffing needs. Moreover, Ireland will need to assess and address high turnover rates within DFAT that affect the level and quality of engagement with partners and to monitor and continue investing in well-being. Finally, DFAT needs to clarify which skills and competencies it requires in-house, and if and how these relate to different staff categories. The model of diplomats, specialists and generalists needs to be kept under management review to ensure the appropriate blend of skills, expertise and capabilities. Implementation of DFAT's human resources strategic action plan and the planned management review are critical opportunities to address these challenges.

Recommendation

9. Ireland should undertake strategic workforce planning to ensure it has the appropriate skills, expertise and capabilities to deliver on its expanding development co-operation objectives.

Secretariat's report

1 Ireland's global efforts for sustainable development

This chapter looks at Ireland's global leadership on issues important to developing countries. It explores Ireland's efforts to ensure that its domestic policies are coherent and in line with the 2030 Agenda for Sustainable Development and its work to raise awareness of global development issues at home.

The chapter first reviews Ireland's efforts to support global sustainable development, assessing its engagement and leadership on global public goods and challenges such as international peace and security, and in promoting global frameworks. It then examines whether Ireland's own policies are coherent with sustainable development in developing countries. The chapter concludes by looking at Ireland's promotion of global awareness of development and citizenship at home.

In brief

Ireland is a successful influencer of global policies on sustainable development, with the ambition to continue playing a significant role in global debates. The international community has adopted important global frameworks thanks to Ireland's effective facilitation. Ireland actively engages in the follow-up to the 2030 agenda. It has clearly defined foreign policy priorities and advocates these effectively.

Ireland is making serious efforts to address policy coherence for sustainable development (PCSD). It has made progress on tax, engages on health worker migration and has consistently supported United Nations peacekeeping operations. But challenges remain, first and foremost in terms of the fight against climate change. Ireland has opportunities to move from ad hoc approaches to PCSD to more systematic assessment, monitoring, and political debate and arbitration. It could make its commitment to PCSD more explicit and use the next national strategy on the Sustainable Development Goals to adopt a structured, cross-government approach.

The Irish population is very supportive of sustainable development, and the government and its partners are well placed to sustain and deepen this support. The government promotes whole-of-society contributions to sustainable development through consultation, outreach and partnerships, in particular with non-governmental organisations. Greater knowledge of global development issues could maintain popular support for sustainable development and co-operation over the long term, as well as building global citizenship. In this regard, increased spending on development awareness would enable Ireland to further reap the benefits of its strong approach to development education. Its new narrative for international development also gives Ireland an opportunity to strengthen its communications on development co-operation.

Ireland is a successful influencer of global policies on sustainable development

The international community has adopted important global frameworks thanks to Ireland's effective facilitation. Ireland co-facilitated, with Kenya, the adoption of the 2030 Agenda for Sustainable Development. It co-facilitated, with Jordan, the New York Declaration for Refugees and Migrants, which paved the way for the adoption of the Global Compacts on migration and refugees. Also noteworthy is Ireland's support to enable the participation of representatives from least developed countries (LDCs) in global framework discussions, particularly in negotiations on the United Nations (UN) Framework Convention on Climate Change and meetings of the Scaling Up Nutrition network and the Commission on the Status of Women.

Ireland intends to continue playing a significant role in global debates. In 2018, Ireland adopted a strategy whereby it aims to double the scope and impact of its global footprint by 2025 (Government of Ireland, 2018[1]), increasing its presence, deepening foreign relations and promoting its values. In its statement on foreign policy, *Global Island*, Ireland identifies as priority values for its foreign policy human rights, peace, and the fight against poverty and hunger (Government of Ireland, 2015[2]).

Ireland actively engages in the follow-up to the 2030 Agenda, integrating domestic and global engagement. Ireland has established monitoring and implementation mechanisms. Its first Voluntary National Review in 2018 also set out a reporting plan until 2030 (Government of Ireland, 2018[3]). In addition, Ireland's Sustainable Development Goal (SDG) National Implementation Plan 2018-2020 assigns Government departments for each of the 169 SDG targets (with the Department of Foreign Affairs and Trade leading on SDG 17) and indicates how key national policies relate to the SDGs (Government of Ireland, 2018[4]). This plan will lay the groundwork for a new national sustainable development strategy that integrates the SDGs.

Ireland advocates successfully on its foreign policy priorities. This advocacy has manifested in Irish leadership at the international level on women, peace and security (Box 1.1 and Chapter 7). Ireland has championed the fight against gender-based violence in humanitarian settings.[1] It is a persistent voice for disarmament and, together with a core group of UN member states, promoted the Treaty on the Prohibition of Nuclear Weapons, again focusing on gender equality.[2] It also spearheaded the adoption of Human Rights Council resolutions on civil society and continuously promotes civic space (Chapter 2).

Box 1.1. Strategic approach to women, peace and security

Ireland's national action plans on women, peace and security are good examples of a strategic approach to addressing a global challenge. In 2011, Ireland adopted its first national action plan to follow-up on UN Security Council Resolution 1325 (adopted in 2000) and subsequent resolutions on women, peace and security. It adopted a second national action plan in 2015 and the third in 2019 (Government of Ireland, 2019[5]). The plan was elaborated in a broad consultation. Among its features are:

- Cross-government engagement. Led by the Department of Foreign Affairs and Trade (DFAT), the Irish engagement also mobilises the Defence Forces to ensure gender-sensitivity in peacekeeping and the Department of Justice and An Garda Siochana (national police) to fight trafficking, sexual exploitation and abuse.
- Multi-level approach. By linking domestic action, Ireland's engagement abroad (development, humanitarian and peace), and its international advocacy in the UN and the European Union (EU), the plan maximises expertise building within Ireland and makes Irish advocacy more compelling.
- Comprehensive approach. The plan relies on the four pillars of prevention, participation, protection and promotion and recognises in particular that more of a focus on prevention is needed.
- Results-orientation. While previous plans underwent a mid-term and final review, the third action plan features a detailed monitoring framework with objectives and performance indicators to ensure effective follow-up, steered by an independently chaired oversight group.

Source: (Government of Ireland, 2019[5]), *Women, Peace and Security: Ireland's Third National Action Plan for the Implementation of UNSCR 1325 and Related Resolutions 2019-2024*, https://www.dfa.ie/media/dfa/ourrolepolicies/womenpeaceandsecurity/Third-National-Action-Plan.pdf.

Policy coherence for sustainable development

Ireland is making serious efforts to address challenges to policy coherence for sustainable development (PCSD). Ireland has made progress on the sensitive issue of taxation, engages on health worker migration and sends many troops to UN peacekeeping operations. But challenges remain. While its domestic policies alone may often not have a sizeable effect on developing countries, Ireland's constructive participation in global frameworks can enhance the effectiveness of those policies and, in turn, influence the behaviour of other states.

Tax and finance. Ireland deserves credit for having undertaken a spill-over analysis in this critical area for its economy and, albeit with a long transition period slowly, phasing out loopholes as part of the OECD and Group of Twenty work on base erosion and profit shifting. It is fully compliant with global tax transparency standards (OECD, 2017[6]), has recently achieved compliance status on anti-money laundering and combatting the financing of terrorism (Financial Action Task Force, 2019[7]), and has made progress on implementing the OECD anti-bribery convention (OECD, 2018[8]). Ireland has signed and ratified the multilateral convention to implement tax treaty-related measures to prevent base erosion and profit shifting (BEPS) and adopted its principal anti-abuse provision.[3] It is also implementing the BEPS treaty related to minimum standards on treaty shopping. Building on the spill-over analysis, Ireland could continue to monitor the effects of its tax policies on revenue collection in developing countries.

Trade and investment. Ireland is increasingly engaging its private sector on responsible business conduct. While implementation of a national action plan on business and human rights (Government of Ireland, 2017[9]) is slow, a baseline study provides useful information on possible areas for improvement, including following other countries in legislating mandatory human rights due diligence in international business transactions (ReganStein, 2019[10]). Ireland could consider strengthening the role of the OECD National Contact Point for responsible business conduct, whose capacity is limited compared to those in other OECD countries (OECD, 2019[11]).

Security: Ireland is the biggest contributor of personnel to UN peacekeeping operations as a proportion of its population among all Development Assistance Committee (DAC) member countries and has an unbroken record of UN peacekeeping service since 1958. Its arms exports are very limited (Wezeman et al., 2019[12]). There is significant demand for export licenses for dual use goods, including to countries engaged in armed conflicts, and the government controls and sometimes denies these (Government of Ireland, 2019[13]).

Health worker migration: Ireland continues to be highly dependent on foreign-trained health professionals, although it trains numerous students (OECD, 2019[14]). These include doctors trained in developing countries such as Pakistan and Sudan that are themselves experiencing shortages of health professionals. To respond to this, Ireland has instituted a training partnership with Pakistan and a more comprehensive partnership with Sudan that reflect health migration between both countries as a whole. Ireland also promotes global collaboration on health worker migration.[4] However, for a high number of foreign-trained junior doctors, Ireland does not provide a career path – leaving them in posts without further training possibilities – despite its commitment to the World Health Organization Global Code of Practice on the International Recruitment of Health Personnel (OECD, 2019[14]).[5]

Forced displacement: In December 2019, Ireland announced to expand its national resettlement programme from 2020 to 2023. A community sponsorship programme launched in 2018 enables private citizens to sponsor resettled refugees. These are welcome steps as Ireland hosts fewer refugees per capita than many DAC members.[6]

Climate change: Ireland is taking steps to step up its contribution in the fight against climate change. A new 2019 climate action plan sets out detailed actions and ambitious emission goals across key policy areas (Government of Ireland, 2019[15]). A proposed Climate Action (Amendment) Bill would legally require the government to set five-year carbon budgets and annual targets for each sector. The government has also announced an increase of the carbon tax, to EUR 26 per tonne, in line with its planned trajectory from EUR 20 in 2019 to EUR 80 in 2030. At present, Ireland is projected to miss its 2020 EU emission targets by a wider margin than almost all other EU member states and, based on mid-2019 projections, it also will not meet its 2030 targets (Environmental Protection Agency, Ireland, 2019[16]). The government estimates that, Ireland will need to buy carbon credits for EUR 6 - 13 million to comply with the 2020 targets. Agriculture is the single most important sector, responsible for one third of emissions. This is mainly due to dairy and beef production; the latter is heavily dependent on commodity-specific support from the EU's Common Agricultural Policy (Climate Change Advisory Council, 2019[17]), (OECD, 2019[18]) that is partially paid by Irish citizens as net contributors to the EU. As Ireland aims to further develop this export-oriented industry, significantly reducing emissions in the sector will be particularly challenging.[7]

Ireland has opportunities to move towards more systematic assessment, monitoring, and political debate and arbitration of policy coherence issues

Ireland needs to make its commitment to PCSD more explicit. Both the new international development policy, *A Better World* (Government of Ireland, 2019[19]), and the SDG National Implementation Plan contain a commitment to coherent government action in development co-operation and in efforts to achieve the SDGs. However, these documents leave open whether this commitment extends to the coherence of

Irish domestic policies with sustainable development abroad and in particular in developing countries. Additionally, further work is needed as to where Ireland sees coherence challenges.

Ireland could establish a specific mechanism for monitoring and assessing transboundary effects of domestic policies. The Department of Communications, Climate Action & Environment and DFAT are joint leads for policy coherence. Terms of reference of interdepartmental bodies for SDG follow-up and international co-operation[8] could usefully include PCSD to ensure these bodies discuss specific coherence challenges. The national SDG stakeholder forum could enable contributions on policy coherence from a broad range of stakeholders. The government could submit progress reports on Policy Coherence for Development to the parliament, as it had committed to do under its previous development co-operation policy, *One World, One Future*.

Ireland could seize opportunities for a structured cross-government approach. The 2014 peer review and a 2018 parliamentary review (Joint Committee on Foreign Affairs and Trade, 2018[20]) recommended that Ireland develop a cross-government plan to address PCSD. Such a plan could identify critical coherence challenges, ensure monitoring of policies, and promote political and societal debate that is necessary for adjustments in sensitive policy areas. A new initiative by the Environmental Protection Agency on SDG interaction, for example, could provide useful information on transboundary effects, and DFAT is also exploring a research project. Encouraging diplomatic missions and embassies to report policy coherence challenges could also result in useful feedback on views in developing countries.

Global awareness

The Irish population is very supportive of sustainable development, and the government and its partners are well placed to sustain and deepen this support

The Irish population has a positive attitude towards development co-operation and acts in support of sustainable development. A higher proportion of people in Ireland than in other EU countries consider it very important to help people in developing countries – 49% compared to 36% across all EU member states (TNS Opinion & Social, 2019[21]) and there is broad, cross-party support for development co-operation. Most Irish respondents to a 2018 Eurobarometer survey said they think they can play a role as an individual in addressing poverty in developing countries (74% versus 53% in the EU) (TNS Opinion & Social, 2018[22]). In a related finding, the share of those giving to charity is much higher than in the EU on average (40% versus 22%). Ireland has a very large fair trade retail market relative to the size of its economy (Fairtrade International, 2018[23]), and volunteering is a strong Irish tradition.

Greater knowledge of global development issues could maintain popular support for sustainable development and co-operation over the long term. The 2015 Global Education Network Europe peer review highlighted that "knowledge about the causes of issues of global poverty and injustice remains sketchy at best" (Global Education Network Europe, 2015[24]). Moreover, only 36% of Irish people responding to a 2017 Eurobarometer poll reported having heard of the SDGs, lower than the EU average (TNS Opinion & Social, 2017[25]). The government deems low awareness of the SDGs in Ireland as a challenge to its policy objectives[9] (Government of Ireland, 2018[3]). Greater knowledge and awareness would likely not only help in making the case for increased official development assistance (Chapter 3). It also could support discussions on policy coherence given thatclimate change, tax policies and health worker migration are issues of great relevance to the Irish population.

Mobilising more funds for development education would allow Ireland to reap the benefits of its strong approach to promoting global citizenship. Ireland has received international recognition for its development education strategies. Actions under the *Irish Aid Development Education Strategy 2017-2023* (Department of Foreign Affairs and Trade, 2017[26]) cover both formal education (by targeting children and students) and non-formal education (by targeting the public at large) (Box 1.2). Awareness-raising activities across children's school careers have an impressive reach.[10] However, without additional investment, Ireland cannot seize the opportunity to help turn development-aware children into development-aware adults who could then contribute in their communities, as consumers, or in politics. For instance, internal performance reporting for 2017 indicates that 6 600 persons were reached through non-formal education, or approximately 1 of every 700 Irish people. New partnerships should help expand reach. While Ireland remains an average DAC funder of development awareness,[11] it commits in *A Better World* to mobilising more resources. This responds as well to strong calls by Irish civil society for greater resources for this.

The government promotes whole-of-society contributions to sustainable development. A National SDG Stakeholder Forum meets regularly to discuss progress on specific goals. DFAT also regularly consults a broad range of stakeholders on its policies, with a prime example being the broad consultation around the development of *A Better World* (Box 2.1). Partnerships with civil society are particularly close (Chapter 5), including on development awareness. However, a new Charities Governance Code aims to improve the governance of all charities in Ireland, including those that seek to promote sustainable development in Ireland and abroad. Regular monitoring and dialogue would enable Ireland to ascertain whether the code strikes the right balance between quality requirements and administrative burden, in particular for smaller organisations. The government's engagement with the private sector on human rights and corporate social responsibility (Chapters 2 and 3) has not yet translated into wider private sector engagement on the SDGs.[12] DFAT also intends to collaborate more with academic institutions (Chapter 5). Outreach to Irish local authorities is still limited.

Its new narrative for international development gives Ireland an opportunity to communicate more effectively on development co-operation. In *A Better World*, Ireland presents a convincing narrative that builds on its history, values and interests (Box 2.1). This resonates with the Irish public, as many Irish people feel that development assistance is in Ireland's self-interest as well as a moral obligation (TNS Opinion & Social, 2018[22]). Ireland now intends to integrate this new narrative in all its communications efforts. This will require close collaboration with civil society partners, as they are central actors in the communication with the Irish public. A new communications strategy will also need to reflect how to add to existing communications and media relations skills in DFAT by building dedicated DFAT capacity for developing content that fits the new narrative. This will also require putting in place mechanisms to encourage and enable missions and units to easily deliver content back to the Communications Unit.

Box 1.2. Ireland's approach to development education

The 2015 Global Education Network Europe peer review praised Ireland as a leader in Europe (Global Education Network Europe, 2015[24]). Ireland used the peer review findings to further improve its strategic approach in its 2017-223 Development Education Strategy (Department of Foreign Affairs and Trade, 2017[26]). Some of the key features of Ireland's approach to development education include:

- Addressing both formal and non-formal education at all ages - Ireland pursues a universal approach, recognising that continuous outreach at various stages of a person's life is much more likely to lead to sustained behaviour change. Curricula in Ireland now reflect development education in various subjects from primary school to the final post-primary exams. Ireland currently works to also raise development awareness in pre-school education. Non-formal education aims to reach youth and adults.

- Investing in partnerships - The Department of Education and Skills (DES) is indispensable in adapting formal education. While there is no single integrated government strategy, increasingly close collaboration ensures that DFAT-funded activities and DES actions work well together. Other key partners are civil society, community organisations such as the National Youth Council and local authorities. Ireland aims to build capacity of partners and incentivises collaboration among organisations through additional funding. The Irish Development Education Association brings together all stakeholders and promotes knowledge exchange and good practices.

- Focusing on results - The development education strategy's detailed performance framework includes outcomes on increased knowledge and behaviour change (Department of Foreign Affairs and Trade, Ireland, 2017[27]). DFAT monitors progress annually. The DES Strategy underwent a mid-term review in 2018 (Department of Education and Skills, Ireland, 2018[28]). A specific research project will assess how different messaging affects the attitudes of diverse audiences in order to track progress and adapt actions.

Source: (Department of Foreign Affairs and Trade, 2017[26]).

References

Climate Change Advisory Council (2019), *Annual Review 2019*, http://www.climatecouncil.ie/media/Climate%20Change%20Advisory%20Council%20Annual%20Review%202019.pdf.   [17]

Department of Education and Skills, Ireland (2018), *Education for Sustainability - The National Strategy on Education for Sustainable Development in Ireland: Report of Interim Review and Action Plan for Q4 2018-Q4 2020*, https://www.education.ie/en/Schools-Colleges/Information/Education-for-Sustainable-Development/Education-for-Sustainable-Development.html.   [28]

Department of Finance, Ireland (2018), *Reservations and Notifications under the Multilateral Convention to Implement Tax Treaty Related Measures to Prevent Base Erosion and Profit Shifting*, http://www.oecd.org/tax/treaties/beps-mli-position-ireland.pdf (accessed on 6 November 2019).   [32]

Department of Foreign Affairs and Trade, Ireland (2017), *Irish Aid Development Education Strategy 2017-2023: Performance Measurement Framework*, https://www.irishaid.ie/media/irishaid/allwebsitemedia/60aboutirishaid/Irish-Aid-DevEd-Strategy-PMF.pdf (accessed on 7 November 2019). [27]

Department of Foreign Affairs and Trade, I. (2017), *Irish Aid Development Education Strategy 2017-2023*, https://www.irishaid.ie/media/irishaid/allwebsitemedia/20newsandpublications/publicationpdfs english/Development-Education-Strategy-2017-2023.pdf (accessed on 7 November 2019). [26]

Environmental Protection Agency, Ireland (2019), *Ireland's Greenhouse Gas Emissions Projections: 2018-2040*, https://www.dccae.gov.ie/en-ie/climate-action/topics/climate-disruption-plan/Pages/default.aspx (accessed on 6 November 2019). [16]

Fairtrade International (2018), *Working Together for Fair and Sustainable Trade: Annual Report 2017-2018*, https://files.fairtrade.net/publications/2017-18_FI_AnnualReport.pdf (accessed on 6 November 2019). [23]

Financial Action Task Force (2019), "Outcomes FATF Plenary, 16-18 October 2019 (webpage)", https://www.fatf-gafi.org/publications/fatfgeneral/documents/outcomes-plenary-october-2019.html (accessed on 6 November 2019). [7]

Global Education Network Europe (2015), *Global Education in Ireland*, https://gene.eu/wp-content/uploads/Gene_NationalReport-Ireland.pdf (accessed on 6 November 2019). [24]

Government of Ireland (2019), *A Better World: Ireland's Policy for International Development*, https://www.irishaid.ie/media/irishaid/aboutus/abetterworldirelandspolicyforinternationaldevelo pment/A-Better-World-Irelands-Policy-for-International-Development.pdf. [19]

Government of Ireland (2019), *Climate Action Plan 2019: To Tackle Climate Breakdown*, https://www.teagasc.ie/media/website/publications/2019/climate-action-plan.pdf (accessed on 6 November 2019). [15]

Government of Ireland (2019), *Report Under the Control of Exports Act 2008, Covering the Period 1st January-31st December 2018*, https://dbei.gov.ie/en/Publications/Publication-files/Report-under-the-Control-of-Exports-Act-2008--2018.pdf (accessed on 6 November 2019). [13]

Government of Ireland (2019), *Women, Peace and Security: Ireland's Third National Action Plan for the Implementation of UNSCR 1325 and Related Resolutions, 2019-2024*, https://www.dfa.ie/media/dfa/ourrolepolicies/womenpeaceandsecurity/Third-National-Action-Plan.pdf. [5]

Government of Ireland (2018), *Global Ireland: Ireland's Global Footprint to 2025*, https://www.ireland.ie/media/ireland/stories/globaldiaspora/Global-Ireland-in-English.pdf. [1]

Government of Ireland (2018), *Ireland: Voluntary National Review 2018*, https://www.dccae.gov.ie/documents/Ireland%20Voluntary%20National%20Review%202018. pdf. [3]

Government of Ireland (2018), *The Sustainable Development Goals National Implementation Plan 2018-2020*, https://www.dccae.gov.ie/documents/DCCAE-National-Implement-Plan.pdf. [4]

Government of Ireland (2017), *National Plan on Business and Human Rights 2017-2020*, https://www.dfa.ie/media/dfa/alldfawebsitemedia/National-Plan-on-Business-and-Human-Rights-2017-2020.pdf (accessed on 6 November 2019). [9]

Government of Ireland (2015), *The Global Island: Ireland's Foreign Policy for a Changing World*, https://www.dfa.ie/media/dfa/alldfawebsitemedia/ourrolesandpolicies/ourwork/global-island/the-global-island-irelands-foreign-policy.pdf. [2]

Joint Committee on Foreign Affairs and Trade, A. (2018), *Review of the Irish Aid Programme*, Houses of the Oireachtas, Dublin, https://data.oireachtas.ie/ie/oireachtas/committee/dail/32/joint_committee_on_foreign_affairs_and_trade_and_defence/reports/2018/2018-02-22_report-review-of-the-irish-aid-programme_en.pdf (accessed on 6 November 2019). [20]

OECD (2019), *Agricultural Policy Monitoring and Evaluation 2019*, OECD Publishing, Paris, https://dx.doi.org/10.1787/39bfe6f3-en. [18]

OECD (2019), *Progress Report on National Contact Points for Responsible Business Conduct*, OECD Publishing, Paris, http://www.oecd.org/mcm/documents/NCPs%20-%20CMIN(2019)7%20-%20EN.pdf (accessed on 6 November 2019). [11]

OECD (2019), *Recent Trends in International Migration of Doctors, Nurses and Medical Students*, OECD Publishing, Paris, https://dx.doi.org/10.1787/5571ef48-en. [14]

OECD (2018), *Implementing the OECD Anti-Bribery Convention - Phase 1bis Report: Ireland*, OECD Publishing, Paris, https://www.oecd.org/corruption/anti-bribery/Ireland-Phase-1bis-Report-ENG.pdf (accessed on 6 November 2019). [8]

OECD (2017), *Global Forum on Transparency and Exchange of Information for Tax Purposes: Ireland 2017 (Second Round) - Peer Review Report on the Exchange of Information on Request*, Global Forum on Transparency and Exchange of Information for Tax Purposes, OECD Publishing, Paris, https://dx.doi.org/10.1787/9789264280229-en. [6]

Popplewell, C. (2017), "Taking the SDGs to where people have fun: Ireland's Electric Picnic Festival", *The SDG Communicator blog*, https://sdg-communicator.org/2017/11/20/taking-the-sdgs-to-where-people-have-fun-irelands-electric-picnic-festival/. [29]

ReganStein (2019), *National Plan on Business and Human Rights: Baseline Assessment of Legislative and Regulatory Framework*, Department of Foreign Affairs and Trade, Dublin, https://www.dfa.ie/media/dfa/ourrolepolicies/internationalpriorities/Baseline-Study---Business-and-Human-Rights.pdf (accessed on 6 November 2019). [10]

TNS Opinion & Social (2019), *Eurobarometer 494: EU Citizens and Development Cooperation*, https://ec.europa.eu/commfrontoffice/publicopinion/index.cfm/Survey/getSurveyDetail/instruments/SPECIAL/surveyKy/2252. [21]

TNS Opinion & Social (2018), *Special Eurobarometer 476: EU Citizens and Development Cooperation*, European Commission, Brussels, https://ec.europa.eu/europeaid/sites/devco/files/ebs-476-report-20180925_en.pdf. [22]

TNS Opinion & Social (2017), *Special Eurobarometer 455: EU Citizens' Views on Development, Cooperation and Aid*, European Commission, Brussels, https://ec.europa.eu/europeaid/sites/devco/files/sp455-development-aid-final_en.pdf. [25]

UNHCR (2018), *Population Statistics - Mid-Year Statistics (database)*, UN Refugee Agency, Geneva, http://popstats.unhcr.org/en/persons_of_concern (accessed on 6 May 2019).   [30]

Wezeman, P. et al. (2019), *Trends in International Arms Transfers*, Stockholm International Peace Research Institute, Solna, Sweden, https://www.sipri.org/sites/default/files/2019-03/fs_1903_at_2018.pdf (accessed on 9 April 2019).   [12]

World Bank (2019), *World Development Indicators (database)*, https://databank.worldbank.org/data/reports.aspx?source=world-development-indicators (accessed on 25 April 2019).   [31]

Notes

[1] Ireland has done so as chair of the Committee on the Status of Women and as donor lead of the UN Office for the Coordination of Humanitarian Affairs and the International Committee of the Red Cross.

[2] Ireland successfully advocated for the reflection of gender equality in the Treaty on the Prohibition of Nuclear Weapons and, with Namibia, co-chairs the International Gender Champions Disarmament Impact Group.

[3] It should be noted that the convention will only apply with respect to bilateral treaties where both parties have signed the convention and listed the treaty. Ireland has not adopted all of the convention's anti-abuse provisions. For instance, Ireland made a reservation to not apply Article 12, which contains the provision that changes the permanent establishment definition and addresses commissionaire arrangements and similar strategies (Department of Finance, Ireland, 2018[32]).

[4] In 2017, Ireland hosted the fourth Global Forum on Human Resources for Health.

[5] If adopted, a proposed Regulated Professions (Health and Social Care) (Amendment) Bill 2019 would allow foreign doctors to be included in a national professional training scheme.

[6] At the end of 2018, Ireland hosted 0.12% refugees per capita, while for example Italy hosted 0.31%, Finland 0.40% and Austria 1.46%. The per capita figure is the author's calculation, based on UNHCR statistics for the end of 2018 (UNHCR, 2018[30]) at http://popstats.unhcr.org/en/persons_of_concern, and population data from the World Development Indicators (World Bank, 2019[31]).

[7] The Climate Change Advisory Council stated in its 2019 annual review: "Emissions in Agriculture are projected to continue increasing to 2030 due to growing cattle numbers, increased fertiliser use and ongoing carbon losses from land. If allowed to proceed unchecked, this would seriously undermine our ability to meet our 2030 target for a reduction in national emissions" (Climate Change Advisory Council, 2019[17]). Under the Climate Action Plan, Ireland foresees to cut emissions in the agriculture sector by 10-15% by 2030, a much lower target than in electricity, transport or built environment (ranging between 40% and 55%) (Government of Ireland, 2019[15]).

[8] An inter-departmental, senior officials group and an inter-departmental working group on the SDGs, and an inter-departmental committee on development co-operation.

[9] In an example of efforts to inform new audiences of the SDGs, Irish Aid presented the SDGs at a large music festival. For more details, see (Popplewell, 2017[29]) at https://sdg-communicator.org/2017/11/20/taking-the-sdgs-to-where-people-have-fun-irelands-electric-picnic-festival/.

[10] In 2017, awareness-raising efforts reached 34% of primary schools, 59% of post-primary schools and 85% of higher education institutions, according to unpublished DFAT data (Department of Foreign Affairs and Trade, Ireland, 2017[27]). The Global Education Network Europe awarded Ireland with one of its 2018 innovation awards for the initiative WorldWise Global Passport. The passport is given to Irish schools in recognition of their engagement on citizenship education.

[11] Ireland spends roughly USD 1 per capita on development awareness (i.e. a total of USD 5 million in 2018). Some DAC members report either significantly higher or significantly lower per capita spending on this. It should be noted that Ireland mobilised much higher funding in the past, but that spending dropped sharply from USD 7.9 million in 2009 and USD 6.7 million in 2013 and to USD 4.2 million in 2015.

[12] For instance, the Irish Business and Employers Confederation, the Irish apex body for businesses, has a campaign on climate change but otherwise does not advocate for sustainable development or the SDGs.

2 Ireland's policy vision and framework

This chapter assesses the extent to which clear political directives, policies and strategies shape Ireland's development co-operation and reflect its international commitments, including the 2030 Agenda for Sustainable Development.

The chapter begins with a look at the policy framework guiding development co-operation, assessing whether Ireland has a clear policy vision that aligns with the 2030 Agenda and reflects its own strengths. It then examines whether Ireland's policy guidance sets out a clear and comprehensive approach, including to poverty. The final section focuses on the decision-making basis, i.e. whether Ireland's policy provides sufficient guidance for decisions about where and how to allocate its official development assistance.

In brief

The 2019 policy for international development, *A Better World*, builds on strong consensus across Irish society and the government. It provides a clear vision for Ireland's development co-operation as a programme that promotes both values and self-interest, aligns with the Sustainable Development Goals, and is rooted in Ireland's foreign policy. Policy priorities are clear and reflect actual strengths, allowing Ireland to add value. *A Better World* puts greater emphasis on cross-cutting issues and on leveraging interlinkages across sectorial interventions. It provides for expanding Ireland's geographical focus, which may create a risk that development programmes may be spread too thin. The policy also includes a commitment to improve the way of working in order for Ireland to become a more dynamic, responsive and effective learning actor.

Reaching the furthest behind first is at the core of *A Better World*, and Ireland is developing a clear and accessible guidance to this approach. Updated strategies and operational guidance on policy priorities is required to ensure that all actions contribute effectively to the achievement of *A Better World*. Mainstreaming of gender equality in policy and programming is advancing. Ireland mainstreams climate adaptation more than the DAC member average in its priority sectors. Nevertheless, new operational guidance and staff capacity-building could help Ireland to further embed a strategic approach to mainstreaming across the board.

Spending targets provide a basis for high-level decision making and a forthcoming Accountability Framework will ensure focus on a manageable number of commitments. At country level, the preparation of mission strategies enables Ireland to make informed choices about its allocations in partner countries. However, further detailing the rationale for partner identification would help staff to guide the choice between possible channels.

Partnerships with civil society are a hallmark of Ireland's development co-operation, exemplifying its global leadership in promoting civic space. At country level, Ireland is a reliable partner to civil society organisations and a recognised lead advocate for civic space. Despite some progress on private sector engagement, Ireland still suffers from the lack of a strategic approach. Its ambition to expand private sector partnerships will benefit from a clearer articulation of scope and risk appetite as part of the new private sector strategy. It will build on its niche in the agri-food sector and show how to deliver across a number of thematic areas. Ireland is a staunch supporter of the multilateral system and considers its membership of the European Union essential to its relations with the rest of the world. Ireland selects and maintains partnerships with multilaterals based on specific criteria and regular reviews, and is developing a Framework for Multilateral Engagement.

Framework

A Better World defines a clear policy vision and is an integral part of Ireland's foreign policy

The 2019 policy for international development, *A Better World,* **provides a clear vision for Ireland's development co-operation and humanitarian assistance** (Government of Ireland, 2019[1]). The new policy marks a noticeable shift in the narrative of Irish official development assistance (ODA), framing it as shared prosperity and self-interest (Box 2.1). The policy envisages development co-operation as "an investment in a better and safer world, in developing new markets, in influence, and in friendships".[1] *A Better World* provides the framework to guide Ireland towards scaling up its international development engagement.

The policy builds on strong consensus and outlines a whole-of-government effort for development co-operation. An extensive consultation with stakeholders that involved citizens, civil society organisations, all government departments and other public bodies contributed to shaping *A Better World* (Department of Foreign Affairs and Trade, Ireland, 2019[2]). This ensured strong buy-in from Irish society as well as government departments beyond the Department of Foreign Affairs and Trade (DFAT). Reflecting the plan to work as a whole of government effort, *A Better World* sets out specific commitments to strengthen co-ordination among different departments on each policy priority (Chapter 4).

A Better World **places the Sustainable Development Goals (SDGs) and responding to the rallying call to reach the furthest behind first at the heart of the Irish approach**. Besides stating resolute support for the SDGs, *A Better World* links each key area of intervention with specific SDGs, showing a clear alignment at goal level with the 2030 Agenda.

A Better World **is solidly rooted in Ireland's foreign policy.** The 2015 foreign policy statement, *The Global Island*, highlights the relevance of development co-operation to Ireland's foreign policy (Government of Ireland, 2015[3]). The 2018 strategy, *Global Ireland,* sets out the ambition to double the country's global footprint by 2025, recognises how development co-operation amplifies and sustains Ireland's place in an interconnected world, and reaffirms the commitment to provide 0.7% of gross national income as ODA by 2030 (Government of Ireland, 2018[4]). Strong support to international rules-based systems and multilateralism is also a pillar of Ireland's foreign policy and thus another key tenet of *A Better World*.

Policy priorities in line with its strengths allow Ireland to add value, but expanded geographical focus risks diluting the effectiveness of Ireland's development co-operation

A Better World **sets a few clear priorities in line with Ireland's strengths that allow it to potentially make a difference in partner countries and at the global level**. The new policy framework puts strong emphasis on four top priorities (gender equality, reducing humanitarian need, climate action and strengthening governance) that cut across Irish development co-operation. It also sets out Ireland's intention to deliver by focusing its action on three clusters of intervention: protection, food and people.[2] As these clusters are in line with previous priority areas, Ireland can build on its experience and on what it is good at and pursue its aim to gain a leadership role in specific policy areas. *A Better World* includes a further commitment to improve the way of doing things to make Ireland a more dynamic, responsive, engaging and effective learning actor (Figure 2.1).

Figure 2.1. Ireland's policy framework for international development in *A Better World*

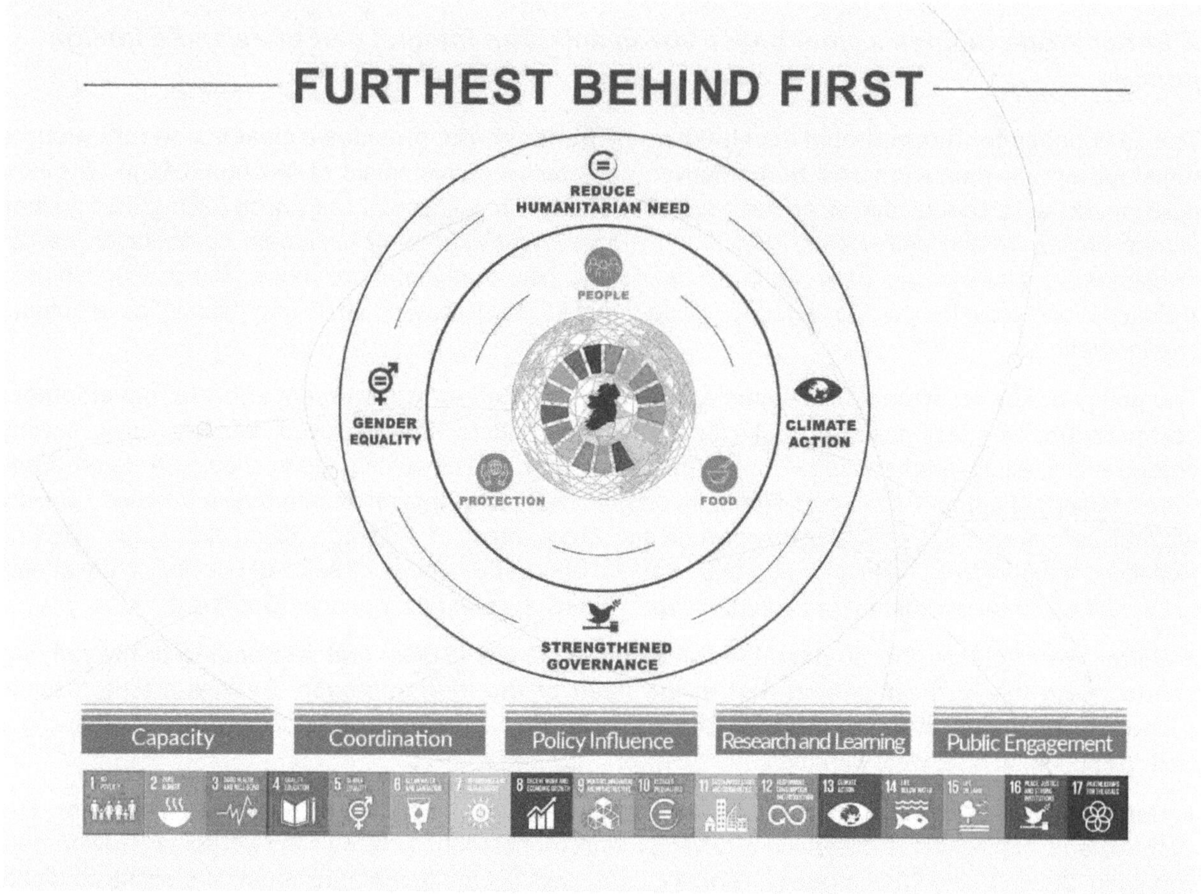

A Better World continues Ireland's focus on Africa and fragile countries and contexts but expands its geographic reach, creating risks for the effectiveness of Ireland's development co-operation. The new policy commits Ireland to consolidate its presence in East and Southern Africa, increase its engagement in West Africa, and expand the support for small island developing states (SIDS).[3] However, it does not provide a clear list of partner countries, as did the previous development policy (Government of Ireland, 2013[5]).[4] Another change is the establishment of new embassies in Jordan and Colombia, the latter as part of Ireland's plans to increase its engagement in South America (Government of Ireland, 2019[6]). This expansion of geographic focus risks diluting Ireland's efforts. It is important that Ireland continues to articulate explicitly how its engagement in new partner countries will add value, especially in places where there is already a large donor presence and Ireland's footprint could be limited. Ireland could draw lessons from its own past experiences, such as when it entered the crowded space in Viet Nam in 2005.[5]

Ireland intends to strengthen its regional approach as a way to increase its footprint and tackle complex issues. It has started to co-operate more with regional institutions and engage in countries of secondary accreditation, including through the Africa Strategy and Innovation Fund (Department of Foreign Affairs and Trade, Ireland, 2018[7]).[6] Global Ireland: Ireland's Strategy for Africa to 2025 (Government of Ireland, 2019[8]) identifies additional regional institutions on the African continent with which Ireland wants to engage. Regional engagement can be a strong complement to bilateral action and help to address challenges that require cross-border co-operation.[7] However, at present, Ireland's regional engagement is still being developed. While it already benefits from enhanced access and a larger footprint, its added value is not yet clear, particularly in terms of Ireland's regional development objectives and links to its country programmes (Annex C).

Box 2.1. An authentic and innovative narrative for development co-operation

A Better World marks a positive shift in Ireland's development co-operation narrative. It successfully combines Ireland's interests and values, telling a convincing story that speaks to the public, civil society and policy makers.

The policy grounds development co-operation both in the traditional solidarity of Irish people and in Ireland's national interest. Although today Ireland is a vibrant economy, the memory of a not-too-distant past marked by poverty and hunger remains vivid. This memory inspires many Irish women and men to dedicate their lives – as missionaries, volunteers and international development workers – to helping some of the poorest and most vulnerable people in the world. The new policy builds on this legacy and frames citizens' support to international co-operation as a projection of Irish values abroad (Chapter 1).

A Better World also recognises that "expanding our overseas development assistance is in Ireland's strategic self-interest".[8] As a small island country with an open economy in an ever more interconnected and uncertain world, Ireland looks at international development co-operation as an essential foreign policy tool to shape and protect its stability and prosperity. In this perspective, supporting internationalism, multilateralism and a rules-based global system is crucial.

Principles and guidance

Reaching the furthest behind first is at the core of A Better World*, but Ireland's approach is yet to be spelled out*

Ireland is strongly committed to reaching the furthest behind first, the overarching goal elaborated in *A Better World*. This pledge to focus development assistance on the poorest and most vulnerable builds on Ireland's traditionally strong focus and commitments that it made in previous development policies.[9]

Ireland is developing a specific approach to reach the furthest behind first. It plans to produce clear and accessible guidance on reaching the furthest behind first by quarter one of 2020. The guidance will contain definitions and strategies for action as well as practical approaches to doing things differently in policy influencing and programming. These will be necessary to support and complement analyses of the local drivers of poverty, inequality and vulnerability that already inform the preparation of new mission strategies (Annex C). It will be essential to invest in new skills and expertise in order to re-orient and strengthen capacities to reach the furthest behind first, as recognised in *A Better World*, and to articulate Ireland's risk appetite to operate in complex contexts (Chapter 4).

Further strategic and operational guidance is needed to translate A Better World*'s vision into action*

Ireland's approach to development co-operation is comprehensive, but further work is needed to update strategic and operational guidance on its policy priorities. Many of the strategies in place date back to the 2000s and need to be updated to reflect the new Irish policy framework and the changed global context. Among the strategies to be refreshed are the policies on gender equality (2004), governance (2008), environment (2008) and civil society (2008). The strategy for partnership with Africa (2019), the strategy for engagement with SIDS (2019) and the social protection strategy (2017) were completed more recently.

Operationalising the policy requires guidance to clarify for partners and staff how the priorities and intervention clusters of *A Better World* interrelate. Ireland plans to complete clear strategies and operational guidance on the four top priorities by the end of 2020. Appropriate sequencing and a roll-out plan for the strategies (with adequate training, support and incentives for staff) will be essential. As observed in Ethiopia, guidance is particularly important during the preparation of new mission strategies to ensure that they substantively align with *A Better World* and contribute to delivering on its vision (Annex C).

Ireland is advancing gender equality, while climate change remains a work in progress

Ireland champions gender equality in policy and programming and wants to build on its progress. Ireland successfully advocates for gender equality and against gender-based violence at global level (Chapter 1) and at country level, as seen in Ethiopia (Annex C). Ireland's efforts to increase investments in gender mainstreaming have been successful. The share of programmes that integrate gender equality (Chapter 3) across its entire portfolio is one of the highest among DAC donors, covering health, education, agriculture and gender-related statistics. Nevertheless, Ireland can still do better. As noted in the *Rapid Overview of One World, One Future* (Department of Foreign Affairs and Trade, Ireland, 2018[9]), Ireland has not been able to fully seize all opportunities due to a lack of additional, dedicated human resources. Reinforcing the DFAT gender network and building capacities on the ground could enhance context analysis and follow-up in programme implementation.[10] *A Better World* elevates gender equality to one of Ireland's top priorities, and Ireland accordingly intends to strengthen its focus further, as seen also in Ethiopia (Annex C).

Ireland's commitment to climate action focuses on adaptation, in line with partner country preferences, but it needs to strengthen staff capacity. The share of ODA focusing on adaptation has steadily improved, registering values higher than the DAC average in Ireland's priority sectors (Figure 3.5). Nevertheless, overall levels of ODA focusing on climate remain low (Chapter 3). In common with other DAC members (OECD, 2019[10]), Ireland also pays limited attention to environmental issues beyond climate change (Chapter 3) and it risks doing so more in the future, as it further concentrates on tackling climate-related issues.[11] Mainstreaming climate across programmes was already a priority under the previous policy. The *Rapid Overview of One World, One Future* recognises that progress in this regard has been uneven – while Ireland invested in partner country capacity, staff and missions need practical support to operationalise this target (Department of Foreign Affairs and Trade, Ireland, 2018[9]). Ireland is now accelerating efforts to mainstream climate action, especially at headquarters level. It created a Climate and Development Learning Platform, publishes annual Climate Action Reports for its partner countries, and provides multi-annual funding to select international climate change partners.[12]

Basis for decision making

Spending targets provide a basis for high-level decision making and a corporate framework will ensure focus on a manageable number of commitments

Ireland uses a number of spending targets to ensure that allocations match priorities. These targets reflect high-level political commitments made in line with top policy priorities such as on climate finance and education.[13] Performance reporting also tracks where aid is spent (e.g. fragile contexts, least developed countries, forgotten crises) and how aid is spent (e.g. channelled through civil society organisations, untied, un-earmarked). In future, Ireland also plans to track spending on the four top policy priorities of *A Better World*. As Ireland moves towards performance budgeting, expected results could provide further evidence to inform allocation decisions.

Ireland is developing an Accountability Framework that will help to keep in focus a manageable number of commitments from *A Better World*. Taking into account lessons learnt from the management framework used under the previous policy, *One World, One Future* (Department of Foreign Affairs and

Trade, Ireland, 2019[11]),[14] Ireland is preparing a new Accountability Framework that will focus on 20-35 high-level commitments from *A Better World*. Identifying lead units and/or divisions and timelines for each commitment, the Accountability Framework will help to track progress on the implementation of the new international development policy (Chapter 6).

Mission strategies help Ireland to make informed decisions

At country level, the preparation of new mission strategies enables Ireland to make informed choices about its allocations in partner countries. A *Standard Approach and Process Guide* sets out the steps required for the development and approval of a mission strategy (Department of Foreign Affairs and Trade, Ireland, 2017[12]). As seen in Ethiopia, these include a thorough process of internal reflection, evaluation of the previous strategy and extensive consultations, as well as an external analysis of the dimensions and drivers of poverty, vulnerability and inequality (Annex C).

The preparation of mission strategies now involves the identification of a broad theory of change, within which Ireland's added value is taken into account and a number of outcomes and associated results are identified. Sectors and programmes in which Ireland has been previously engaged play a significant role in the decision-making process, and the five-year budget plans for mission strategies reflect historic levels of allocations as well as the embassy's absorption capacity. However, missions are now in the position to make more strategic choices around engaging in new sectors or changing the way they are engaging in current sectors. In the past, previous mission strategies were more prescriptive and could reference specific partners, limiting adaptability during the strategy period.

The rationale for selecting partners is not sufficiently detailed to guide allocations

***A Better World* sets out, in broad strokes, why Ireland engages with different actors**. In particular, it stresses the importance of partnerships with civil society and multilaterals and the intention to expand engagement with the private sector and research institutes. However, while it plans to update its civil society policy, Ireland lacks guidance on its partnership with multilaterals and the private sector. The *Research Strategy 2015-2019* is under review to inform an expanded approach to research, evidence, knowledge and learning, together with the associated operational guidance (Ministry of Foreign Affairs and Trade, Ireland, 2015[13]).

Guidance can help Ireland to choose between possible channels and, in particular, to consider the advantages and challenges of a particular channel in a given context.[15] If Irish ODA is to grow, guidance will be especially important because Ireland will need to consider the absorption capacity of specific channels and partners over time, as well as which partners are best placed to work with Ireland in new areas.

Ireland applies clear criteria when identifying partners through competitive selections, but not all partners are selected competitively. Calls for proposals and performance-based partnership arrangements such as the Civil Society Fund, the Programme Grant II and the Humanitarian Programme Plan apply clearly identified criteria, ranging from partner capacity to the quality of proposals and expected results (Department of Foreign Affairs and Trade, Ireland, 2017[14]). Similarly, international funding arrangements initiated by DFAT headquarters, such as the Multi Annual Funding Framework for International Partnerships on Climate Change, apply clear criteria to promote engagement with selected partners. However, at country level, although the Standard Approach to Grant Management (SAGM) provides a set of criteria for selecting partners (Department of Foreign Affairs and Trade, Ireland, 2017[15]),[16] there is no requirement to document if alternative partners were considered, and if not, why not. Ireland can accept unsolicited fund requests and contract partners directly, after having assessed their capacity to deliver. Not scanning the horizon for other potential partners might have drawbacks, such as lower value for money, if partners feel that funding is likely regardless of value added or strong performance.

Partnerships with civil society are a hallmark of Ireland's development co-operation, exemplifying its global leadership in promoting civic space

Vigorous support for Irish as well as local civil society organisations (CSOs) and civic space is a particular feature of Ireland's development co-operation. In line with the 2030 Agenda, *A Better World* emphasises the protection of human rights; the role of CSOs in supporting accountable, well-functioning societies; and the importance of inclusive, participatory and representative institutions. Ireland also is a long-time champion and active defender of civic space and human rights, proactively harnessing strategic opportunities at the global policy level.[17]

At country level, Ireland is a reliable partner to CSOs and a recognised lead advocate for civic space, as seen in Ethiopia (Annex C). Its principled approach ensures the necessary support to CSOs that advocate for civic space, providing a lifeline at times for grassroots campaigns in contexts where civic space is under particular threat. This is especially important in contexts where progress is difficult and hard-won gains can easily be lost. Ireland is recognised for its ability to mobilise key partners around the civic space agenda through effective civil society programmes and projects, often in partnerships with like-minded donors, and through policy dialogue. Ireland is also perceived as a partner that does not shy away from addressing complex civic space issues, including at the highest political level.

Ireland's ambition to expand private sector partnerships would benefit from a clearer articulation of scope and risk appetite

Ireland's private sector engagement still suffers from the lack of a strategic approach that clearly articulates its niche. The 2014 peer review recommended a policy and tools be developed for effective private sector engagement (PSE). In response, Ireland undertook a strategic review that identified a series of possible priorities (Holzman, Barot and Franklin, 2019[16]) and stepped up its engagement in a range of areas (Chapter 3). The agri-food sector has been identified and utilised as a sphere for PSE as it has the potential to deliver transformative development impacts across a number of thematic areas including climate action, women's economic empowerment, inclusive economic growth, nutrition and sustainable food systems. The new strategy for PSE and private finance, currently under development, will be an opportunity to transform what is still a nascent and ad hoc engagement into more systematic partnerships with a clear rationale (Chapter 5). For this, the PSE strategy should clarify the government's risk appetite and help identify new opportunities for collaboration. The PSE strategy could also provide guidance on Ireland's facilitating and matchmaking roles in partner countries, as well as on integrating PSE across different partnerships (e.g. civil society partnerships and engagement through multilaterals) and policy areas (e.g. emphasis on women's economic empowerment and climate action). As a relative newcomer in this area, Ireland can benefit from the diverse experience of other DAC members, development banks, and platforms such as the Donor Committee for Enterprise Development or the Aspen Network of Development Entrepreneurs, as well as the Kampala Principles of the Global Partnership for Effective Development Co-operation (GPEDC, 2019[17]).

Ireland could add specific value by focusing on those at risk of being left behind, in line with *A Better World*. Ireland is well placed to deepen work with Irish and local private partners in sectors where Ireland wants to focus its engagement, notably agri-food but also other sectors where specific programmes could expand, for example in healthcare/pharmaceuticals, energy, education and fintech. The recent review of PSE modalities suggests the need to learn more about the developmental impact of mobilisation efforts, in particular with regard to reaching the most vulnerable (Holzman, Barot and Franklin, 2019[16]). Building on lessons from its programmes,[18] Ireland could help to show that private sector engagement can drive change that benefits marginalised and vulnerable groups.

Ireland supports multilaterals out of strategic interest, but does not yet have a formal strategy

Ireland is a staunch supporter of the multilateral system. *A Better World* explains Ireland's deep commitment to multilateralism, noting that as a small open economy, Ireland relies on a stable and rules-based global system to protect its interests. Ireland has the ambition to increase its policy influence and engages in joint efforts to increase the effectiveness of the multilateral system (Chapter 5). Multilaterals are also a means to increase Ireland's global footprint. In this vein, Ireland is expanding partnerships with development banks, having joined the Asian Infrastructure Investment Bank in 2017 and joining the African Development Bank in 2020.[19]

Ireland considers its membership of the European Union (EU) essential to its relations with the rest of the world, and it intends to contribute even more actively to shaping European external engagement. Due to a foreseen substantial increase of its contribution to the EU multi-annual financial framework 2021-27, Ireland is planning to maximise its influence on the EU by building a system of management, engagement, cross-department collaboration, monitoring and evaluation (Department of Foreign Affairs and Trade, Ireland, 2019[18]) to push for a greater focus on fragile contexts and the furthest behind. This will also bring new opportunities for CSOs supported by Ireland to engage more systematically in relevant dialogue structures at the EU level. Dóchas and DFAT can help in raising awareness about specific entry points for dialogue among Irish CSOs.

Ireland selects and maintains partnerships with multilaterals based on specific criteria and regular reviews, which also guide its allocations for core funding. It partners mainly with multilateral organisations with mandates that are aligned with its own policy priorities and bilateral co-operation programme. Ireland also assesses organisations based on their results and its own capacity to influence them. In addition, *A Better World* specifies how Ireland plans to use multilateral partnerships under each policy priority. Ireland also uses assessments of the Multilateral Organisation Performance Assessment Network and other sources such as the United Kingdom's Multilateral Development Review to regularly adjust its funding decisions (Department for International Development, United Kingdom, 2016[19]). As Ireland plans to increase the aid budget, deepening its investment in priority organisations, including through core resources, could strengthen its voice, which is already valued for its constructive engagement (Chapter 5).

Ireland is developing a Framework for Multilateral Engagement. Ireland's 2014 peer review recommended that the Irish government set out its ambition and priorities for multilaterals. Ireland is in the advanced stages of developing a Framework for Multilateral Engagement that aims to bring a more coherent, holistic and focused approach to multilateral engagement (Department of Foreign Affairs and Trade, Ireland, 2019[11]). This will help Ireland to focus its contributions more strategically and gain greater influence, including through increased collaboration across government departments.

References

Department for International Development, United Kingdom (2016), *Raising the Standard: The Multilateral Development Review 2016*, https://www.gov.uk/government/publications/raising-the-standard-the-multilateral-development-review-2016. [19]

Department of Foreign Affairs and Trade, Ireland (2019), *A Better World Consultation Process Review (internal document)*. [2]

Department of Foreign Affairs and Trade, Ireland (2019), *Implementation of A Better World: Status Report October 2019 (internal document)*. [11]

OECD DEVELOPMENT CO-OPERATION PEER REVIEWS: IRELAND 2020 © OECD 2020

Department of Foreign Affairs and Trade, Ireland (2019), *The Potential Impact of the EU Budget 2021-27 on Ireland's Official Development Assistance and Implication for DFAT (internal document).* [18]

Department of Foreign Affairs and Trade, Ireland (2018), *Mission Guidelines for Africa Strategy and Innovation Fund (internal document).* [7]

Department of Foreign Affairs and Trade, Ireland (2018), *Rapid Overview of One World, One Future (internal document).* [9]

Department of Foreign Affairs and Trade, Ireland (2017), *Appraisers' Guide for the Programme Grant II (2017-2022) and the Humanitarian Programme Plan (2017-2018) (internal document).* [14]

Department of Foreign Affairs and Trade, Ireland (2017), *Standard Approach & Process Guide to Mission Strategy Planning (internal document).* [12]

Department of Foreign Affairs and Trade, Ireland (2017), *Standard Approach to Grant Management in DCAD.* [15]

Government of Ireland (2019), *A Better World: Ireland's Policy for International Development*, https://www.irishaid.ie/media/irishaid/aboutus/abetterworldirelandspolicyforinternationaldevelopment/A-Better-World-Irelands-Policy-for-International-Development.pdf. [1]

Government of Ireland (2019), *DAC Peer Review 2020: Memorandum of Ireland.* [6]

Government of Ireland (2019), *Global Ireland: Ireland's Strategy for Africa to 2025*, Department of Foreign Affairs and Trade, Dublin, https://www.dfa.ie/media/dfa/publications/Global-Ireland---Irelands-Strategy-for-Africa-to-2025.pdf. [8]

Government of Ireland (2018), *Global Ireland: Ireland's Global Footprint to 2025*, https://www.ireland.ie/media/ireland/stories/globaldiaspora/Global-Ireland-in-English.pdf. [4]

Government of Ireland (2015), *The Global Island: Ireland's Foreign Policy for a Changing World*, https://www.dfa.ie/media/dfa/alldfawebsitemedia/ourrolesandpolicies/ourwork/global-island/the-global-island-irelands-foreign-policy.pdf. [3]

Government of Ireland (2014), *Framework for Action for One World, One Future*, https://www.irishaid.ie/media/irishaid/allwebsitemedia/20newsandpublications/publicationpdfsenglish/Action-Framework-Web-Version.pdf. [20]

Government of Ireland (2013), *One World, One Future: Ireland's Policy For International Development*, https://www.irishaid.ie/news-publications/publications/publicationsarchive/2013/may/one-world-one-future-irelands-policy/. [5]

GPEDC (2019), *Kampala Principles on Effective Private Sector Engagement in Development Co-operation*, Global Partnership for Effective Development Co-operation (GPEDC), Paris, https://effectivecooperation.org/wp-content/uploads/2019/06/Kampala-Principles-final.pdf. [17]

Holzman, C., C. Barot and S. Franklin (2019), *A Review of Private Sector Engagement for Development: Recommendations For Ireland*, unpublished. [16]

Ministry of Foreign Affairs and Trade, Ireland (2015), *Irish Aid Research Strategy 2015-2019*, https://www.irishaid.ie/media/irishaid/allwebsitemedia/20newsandpublications/publicationpdfs english/Irish-Aid-Research-Strategy-2015-2019.pdf. [13]

OECD (2019), *Greening Development Co-operation: Lessons from the OECD Development Assistance Committee*, OECD Publishing, Paris, https://doi.org/10.1787/62cc4634-en. [10]

OECD (2019), *OECD Development Co-operation Peer Reviews: Norway 2019*, OECD Development Co-operation Peer Reviews, OECD Publishing, Paris, https://doi.org/10.1787/75084277-en. [22]

OECD (2019), *OECD Development Co-operation Peer Reviews: Switzerland 2019*, OECD Development Co-operation Peer Reviews, OECD Publishing, Paris, https://doi.org/10.1787/9789264312340-en. [23]

OECD (2015), *OECD Development Co-operation Peer Reviews: New Zealand 2015*, OECD Development Co-operation Peer Reviews, OECD Publishing, Paris, https://doi.org/10.1787/9789264235588-en. [21]

Notes

[1] This description is in the Foreword of the policy document by An Tánaiste and Minister for Foreign Affairs and Trade, Simon Coveney.

[2] The protection cluster includes work on fragility, conflict and protracted crises through improved government co-ordination, regional approaches and assistance during emergencies. The food cluster includes work on hunger and/or undernutrition, agricultural markets and inclusive economic growth around agriculture. The protection cluster includes work on health, education and social protection systems.

[3] Support for SIDS will mainly strengthen policy engagement and coherence, building on what done to support SIDS in multilateral processes, with limited financial implications for Ireland especially related to addressing climate vulnerability.

[4] A list of partner countries is published on its website, though not fully up to date. Currently, Ireland's priority countries are Ethiopia, Malawi, Mozambique, Tanzania, Uganda, Zambia, Sierra Leone and Vietnam.

[5] Ireland could also draw on the experience of other DAC members. One such example is New Zealand, which, outside the Pacific, focuses on niche areas rather than trying to work in areas already covered by other donors, thus supporting division of labour. See (OECD, 2015[21]) at https://doi.org/10.1787/9789264235588-en.

[6] The budget of the Africa Strategy and Innovation Fund is EUR 3.5 million in 2019.

[7] Ireland could draw on other DAC members' experience in using regional programmes. For example, Switzerland and Norway engage extensively at regional level. See (OECD, 2019[23]) at https://doi.org/10.1787/9789264312340-en regarding Switzerland and (OECD, 2019[22]) at https://doi.org/10.1787/75084277-en regarding Norway.

[8] See the Foreword written by An Tánaiste and Minister for Foreign Affairs and Trade, Simon Coveney TD, in (Government of Ireland, 2019, p. ii[1]) at https://www.irishaid.ie/media/irishaid/aboutus/ abetterworldirelandspolicyforinternationaldevelopment/A-Better-World-Irelands-Policy-for-International-Development.pdf.

[9] Both the 2006 *White Paper on Irish Aid* and the 2013 document, *One World, One Future*, placed the reduction of poverty and vulnerability at the centre of the Irish international development programme. The 2013 policy, in particular, had as a focus the poorest of the poor.

[10] DFAT Gender Network seeks to support co-ordination, learning and knowledge sharing among gender focal points in headquarters and missions.

[11] Programme agreements include a standard clause obliging implementing partners to contribute towards the promotion and protection of the environment (Chapter 4). Despite this, the Standard Appraisal, Recommendation and Approval form was amended in July 2019 and now assesses programme design against climate action rather than environmental impact.

[12] The Climate and Development Learning Platform, jointly managed by DFAT and the International Institute for Environment and Development, aims to support units and partners to integrate climate change into development programming. See https://www.climatelearningplatform.org. The Climate Action Reports contain information on Ireland's efforts on adaptation and mitigation in partner countries. International climate change partners work to improve the linkages between local experience and international policy frameworks.

[13] For example, at the 2015 United Nations Climate Change Conference, the Taoiseach committed to invest USD 175 million in climate finance by 2020, a target that was reached in 2018. At the United Nations General Assembly in 2018, Ireland committed to provide at least EUR 250 million to global education with a focus on girls and emergencies by 2024. *A Better World* also reports this pledge.

[14] The Framework for Action (Government of Ireland, 2014[20]), used under *One World, One Future*, detailed as many as 150 priority actions under 7 priority areas, which was burdensome and undercut its function as a management instrument.

[15] For instance, how does Ireland conceive the roles of the public sector and civil society in service delivery-heavy sectors such as health and education and of public and private sector in agriculture? What are Ireland's expectations of multilateral organisations and international CSOs in this regard?

[16] According to the SAGM, examples of identification criteria that grant managers have to use when screening potential engagements are: contribution to Ireland's foreign policy objectives; response to needs; partner's capacity and efficiency; presence of historical or outstanding issues with partner; availability of resources; opportunity for learning; etc.

[17] For instance, in the context of the Human Rights Council, Ireland was as co-facilitator of the first United Nations resolutions on civil society space. It is also currently co-chairing the Task Team on Civil Society Development Effectiveness and Enabling Environment.

[18] Examples of such programmes include the Africa Agri-Food Development Programme, the Irish Potato Coalition, and the market and value chain analysis the Coalition has been conducting.

[19] Ireland joined the Asian Development Bank in 2006.

3 Ireland's financing for development

This chapter looks at Ireland's official development assistance (ODA) figures, including the overall level and components of aid, the level of bilateral and multilateral aid, and geographic and sector allocations of bilateral aid. In line with commitments in the Addis Ababa Action Agenda and the emerging concept of total official support for sustainable development, it also examines Ireland's efforts to mobilise finance for sustainable development other than ODA.

The chapter begins with a review of Ireland's ODA volumes and its efforts to meet domestic and international ODA targets. It then discusses the extent to which Ireland allocates bilateral aid according to its statement of intent and international commitments, and examines the effectiveness of Ireland's use of multilateral aid channels. The chapter concludes with a review of financing for sustainable development and how Ireland promotes and catalyses development finance other than ODA.

In brief

Ireland's strong political commitment to reach 0.7% of gross national income (GNI) as official development assistance (ODA) is at risk of remaining unfulfilled. Since 2015, ODA volumes increased but the ODA ratio has stagnated, standing at 0.31% of GNI in 2018, despite a commitment to increase the ratio during periods of economic growth. Strong political support offers an opportunity to move in the right direction, but this requires a plan for when and how to increase spending and a commensurate investment in necessary capacities.

Ireland bilateral aid is well focused. Concentrating on its priority countries in sub-Saharan Africa, Ireland stands out for allocating a high share of its aid to least developed countries (nearly meeting the commitment of 0.15% of GNI) and to fragile states and contexts. Growing the ODA budget is an opportunity for Ireland to increase its financial weight in priority countries in line with its policy influence. Allocations fully match priority sectors and themes, as does the large share of funding to and through civil society organisations.

Multilateral aid is central to Irish development co-operation and plays an increasingly important role. It is also of high quality, with significant voluntary core funding and the use of multi-donor pooled funds where it is earmarked. Ireland's good focus on its priority organisations could translate also into greater financial weight if the ODA budget grows.

Ireland's financial instruments to mobilise private finance are limited to date. As its ambitions are growing, Ireland also aims to improve the development relevance of private finance, including through its influence in multilateral settings and in areas where Ireland has specific expertise. A new, whole-of-government approach provides momentum to help strengthen tax systems and domestic revenue mobilisation in partner countries.

Overall ODA volume

Strong political commitment to reach the ratio of 0.7% GNI to ODA is at risk of remaining unfulfilled although ODA volume has grown

Ireland has yet to deliver on its political commitment to increase its ODA ratio. The full effects of the financial crisis hit Ireland at a time when ODA had been expanding, leading to a very significant decline of the ODA/GNI ratio from 0.59% in 2008 to 0.51% in 2011 and 0.38% in 2014. Between 2015 and 2018, ODA volumes increased from USD 727 million to USD 891 million (constant 2017 prices) – still below its pre-crisis peak in 2008 (USD 1 042 million).[1] Despite this growth in the ODA budget, ODA as a share of GNI did not catch up with the sustained performance of Ireland's economy. In fact, ODA relative to GNI has stagnated since 2015. It stood at 0.31% in 2018 (Figure 3.1), the same value it is projected to stand at in 2020, based on current budget projections. This contrasts with the commitment under the previous development policy, *One World, One Future*, to increase the ODA/GNI ratio when economic growth would resume.

Figure 3.1. ODA as a share of GNI has not grown in line with the economic recovery

Disbursements, 2017 constant prices

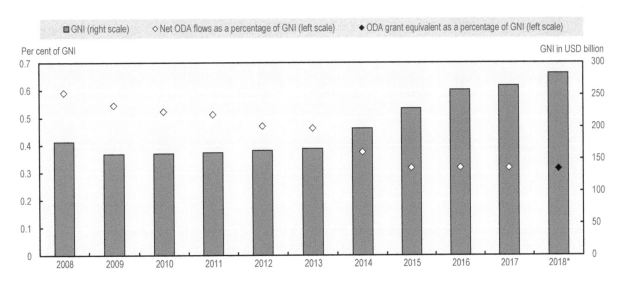

Note: * ODA as a percentage of GNI is in grant equivalents basis.
Source: (OECD, 2019[1]), *Creditor Reporting System* (database), https://stats.oecd.org/Index.aspx?DataSetCode=crs1 (accessed November 2019).

StatLink ᵃᵢₛᐧ https://doi.org/10.1787/888934121126

Strong political support offers an opportunity to live up to Ireland's 0.7% commitment but doing so will require a detailed plan. In *A Better World*, Ireland reiterates its firm commitment to reach 0.7% of GNI as ODA by 2030. The intent to expand development co-operation permeates the entire policy. In its efforts, the government can build on strong bipartisan support in the Joint Committee on Foreign Affairs and Trade, and Defence (2018[2]), which has called on the government to take action on the 0.7% commitment in its 2018 review. However, reaching a 0.7% ratio of ODA/GNI would mean tripling the current aid budget by 2030 – a massive challenge and all the more so in the face of economic uncertainty around Brexit. *A Better World* rightly recognises the need to increase capacity as a priority. In addition to projected annual increases of EUR 100-150 million, a significantly increased aid budget will require a plan that:

- identifies specifically where and when spending can grow
- sets out how to adapt structures, systems and capabilities to deliver and maintain quality
- foresees an advocacy strategy to make a case for annual increases vis-à-vis parliamentarians and the public at large
- incorporates scenarios to reflect economic uncertainty while enabling regular increases.

Figure 3.2. Since 2016, Ireland's ODA allocated to and through multilaterals is trending upward while ODA allocated to and through CSOs and other bilateral ODA has remained stable

Gross disbursements, millions USD, 2017 constant prices

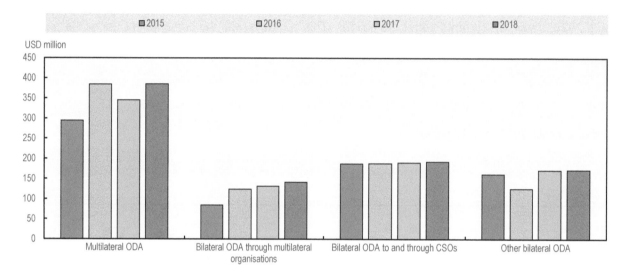

Source: Based on data from (OECD, 2019[1]), *Creditor Reporting System* (database), https://stats.oecd.org/Index.aspx?DataSetCode=crs1 (accessed November 2019).

StatLink 🖳 https://doi.org/10.1787/888934121145

Ireland implements DAC recommendations on aid quality but could improve reporting. By providing 100% of its aid as grants, Ireland meets the recommendation on terms and conditions of aid in regard to respecting the debt capacity of recipient countries. Ireland also provides almost all of its aid untied[2] and advocates for greater progress on this internationally. While Ireland declares its entire portfolio as untied and statistical reporting to the OECD is of good quality, its description of some data (OECD DAC, 2019[3]) as well as transparency (Chapter 5) could be improved.

Bilateral ODA allocations

Ireland focuses its bilateral aid on its geographic and thematic priorities, almost reaching the UN target of allocating 0.15% of ODA/GNI to least developed countries

Focusing on its priority countries in sub-Saharan Africa, Ireland stands out for allocating high shares of its ODA to least developed countries (LDCs) and fragile countries and contexts. Ireland's eight priority countries are consistently among its top ten ODA recipients, along with crisis-affected countries for which Ireland mobilises humanitarian assistance (Table B.3). However, Ireland's share of unallocated bilateral aid has increased significantly in recent years (from 34% in 2013-2014 to 49% in 2017-2018), while the share of aid allocated to the top ten recipients dropped over the same period (from

41% to 29%). The increase of unallocated bilateral ODA mainly related to Ireland having started reporting in-donor refugee costs. Ireland provides 75% of its country allocable aid to LDCs, compared to the DAC average of 39% (Table B.3). Together with its imputed multilateral aid, this corresponds to 0.14% of Ireland's GNI, which is slightly below Ireland's international commitment of 0.15% of GNI to ODA but well above the DAC average of 0.09% (Table B.7). Among DAC members, Ireland is also the donor that allocates the largest share of its allocable bilateral ODA to fragile countries and contexts (55% in 2018, against a DAC average of 35%).

If ODA grows, there is potential to increase Ireland's financial weight in line with its policy influence. Most countries now receiving development co-operation from Ireland have a very significant donor presence. This means that Ireland's ODA represents a relatively small share of total aid received in all of its priority countries and about 1% of total ODA in most of these countries. Only in Sierra Leone is Ireland among the top ten donors (Figure 3.3). At the same time, Ireland plays a very constructive role even in such contexts (Chapter 5, Annex C). An increased budget could further bolster Ireland's influence in its partner countries. If Ireland chooses to engage in new partner countries, it can be useful to consider its potential added value as a donor; ODA can be an indication of this. This would also match Ireland's commitment to supporting those furthest behind. For its humanitarian assistance, Ireland already follows the good practice of targeting ODA to forgotten crises (in addition to providing valuable core support).

Figure 3.3. Ireland is not a main ODA provider in its top ten partner countries

2016-17 averages

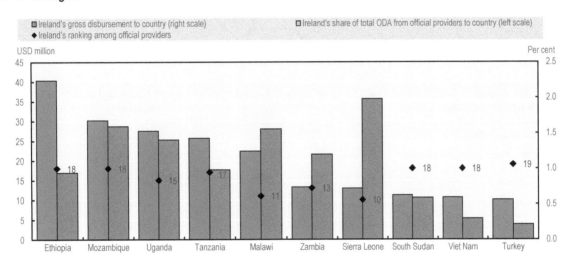

Note: Private development finance from philanthropy is excluded. The order of partner countries is based on gross disbursements of aid received from Ireland.
Source: Based on data from (OECD, 2019[1]), *Creditor Reporting System* (database), https://stats.oecd.org/Index.aspx?DataSetCode=crs1 (accessed November 2019).

StatLink 🖳 https://doi.org/10.1787/888934121164

Ireland's allocations align well with its priorities, with the exception of climate change. The ODA portfolio has a strong thematic focus on human development, governance and civil society, humanitarian assistance, and agriculture – all of the intervention areas identified in *A Better World* (Table B.5). Ireland has also succeeded in massively increasing its share of commitments targeting gender equality and women's empowerment from 46% in 2013-14 to 80% in 2017-18 (Figure 3.4). At the same time, 23% of Irish bilateral, allocable aid supports the environment, compared to a DAC average of 33% in 2017. Despite significant efforts, the share of climate-relevant actions has progressed only moderately, from 17% in

2013-14 to 22% in 2017-18 (Chapter 2; Table B.5). However, mainstreaming climate change in a portfolio focused on social infrastructure and services is less straightforward than for programmes on agriculture or energy. In fact, Ireland's share of adaptation-marked programmes is already higher than the DAC average in all its priority sectors (Figure 3.5). Ireland could explore further the potential to reflect climate change in health and/or social protection and to screen more programmes. Ireland plans to increase its climate contributions through more targeted global and regional initiatives, such as with small island developing states in the Pacific and the Caribbean.

Figure 3.4. Ireland mainstreams gender equality and women's empowerment across all sectors

2017

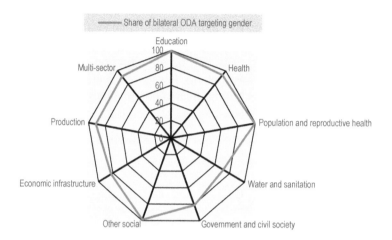

Note: The figure is based on commitments of Ireland's bilateral, sector-allocable aid that have gender equality and women's empowerment as a principal or significant objective.
Source: Based on data from (OECD, 2019[1]), *Creditor Reporting System* (database), https://stats.oecd.org/Index.aspx?DataSetCode=crs1 (accessed November 2019).

StatLink ᵐˢ🔗 https://doi.org/10.1787/888934121183

Figure 3.5. Ireland mainstreams climate change adaptation more than the DAC member average in its priority sectors

Share of total bilateral allocable ODA marked as targeting climate change adaptation as a principal or significant objective, 2016-17

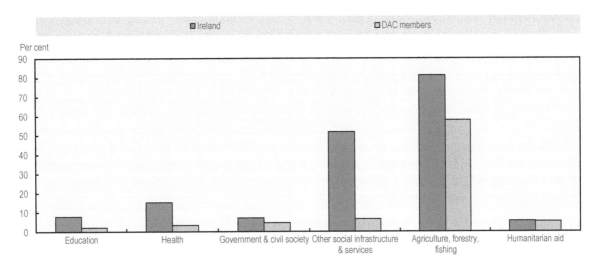

Note: The selected sectors are those where Ireland spends most of its aid. Percentages are based on commitments.
Source: Based on data from (OECD, 2019[1]), *Creditor Reporting System* (database), https://stats.oecd.org/Index.aspx?DataSetCode=crs1 (accessed November 2019).

StatLink 🔗 https://doi.org/10.1787/888934121202

In line with its policy, Ireland's share of bilateral ODA allocated to and through civil society organisations (CSOs) is one of the highest among DAC members, at 38% in 2018. This benefits mainly Irish non-governmental organisations (NGOs), which received 64% of total CSO funding between 2015 and 2018. Country-based development NGOs received 9% and international CSOs received 26% of the total. Among DAC members, Ireland is consistently providing the highest share of bilateral ODA allocated to CSOs (i.e. core contributions that are programmed by CSOs) – 23% in 2018 compared to a DAC average of 2%. The share of Irish bilateral ODA implemented through multilateral organisations is increasing. Conversely, the share of Ireland's government-to-government co-operation is much smaller than that of other DAC members, due to challenging contexts in some partner countries and the phasing out of general budget support as a delivery mechanism. While this could raise questions regarding Ireland's outlook on development effectiveness, in fact, the share of Ireland's development co-operation allocated through public sector channels in some of its priority countries is higher than or similar to the DAC average.

Multilateral ODA allocations

Irish multilateral funding is of high quality and is growing in importance

Multilateral ODA is central to Irish co-operation and plays an increasingly important role. The share of Ireland's aid to multilateral organisations has grown from 36.4% of its total ODA in 2014 to 43.2% 2018[3] (Figure 3.2), mainly because Ireland's assessed contributions to the European Union budget over the period increased. At the same time, Ireland's share of bilateral aid implemented through multilateral organisations grew from 19.5% in 2014 to 27.0% in 2018,[4] as Ireland increased humanitarian spending for country-pooled fund mechanisms. The total share of Irish aid implemented by multilaterals thus rose from

48.7% to 58.6% over this four-year period. While fully acknowledging the importance of Ireland's multilateral engagement, the parliamentary joint committee underscored the need to ensure the effectiveness of this largest part of Irish ODA. *A Better World*, reflects the committee's recommendation (Chapters 2 and 5).

Ireland's multilateral funding is of high quality. Beyond assessed contributions, Ireland's main modality for partnership with its priority multilateral partners is through voluntary core funding. In addition, its multi-bi funding includes multiple regional and country-based pooled funds. This contributes to a co-ordinated response rather than making donor co-ordination more challenging by imposing tight earmarks.

Ireland has a good focus on its priority organisations. From 2014-17, ten organisations accounted for 79.4% of total allocations. The European Union (EU) is by far the most important multilateral channel (60%). Other main partners are United Nations (UN) agencies with mandates that match Ireland's priorities on responding to humanitarian needs, gender equality, food security and human development and also the World Bank. Ireland's ambition to expand the geographic focus of its ODA and pursue regional approaches (Chapter 2) has translated into membership of the Asian Infrastructure Investment Bank in 2017 and the African Development Bank in 2020. However, overall allocations to regional institutions outside Europe remain very limited (Chapter 2).

Maintaining a good focus in ODA increases could raise Ireland's financial weight in priority organisations. With a share of 0.5 - 1.5% of DAC member contributions (2014-17 average), Ireland is a relatively small donor to most of its priority multilateral organisations, as most organisations have very large budgets. Exceptions to this are its contributions to the Central Emergency Response Fund, country-based pooled funds and the Office of the UN High Commissioner for Human Rights. While Ireland's share of core-funding is slightly higher, only its core funding to the World Food Programme, at 6.1% of all DAC donor core funding, stands out.

Financing for sustainable development

Ireland's financial instruments to mobilise private finance are limited to date

Ireland's bilateral use of blended finance instruments has been marginal to date. Ireland has started to leverage ODA to mobilise additional development finance through co-financing with the private sector. However, this is at small scale (amounting to only USD 3.6 million in 2017) and concentrated on the Africa Agri-Food Development Programme (AADP), which is run together with the Department of Agriculture, Food and the Marine.[5] Additional, smaller initiatives and engagement through partnerships with others are also growing. These include a catalytic fund set up by the Embassy of Ireland in Kenya; the private sector arms of Irish NGOs such as Vita's Green Impact Fund and the work by Self-Help Africa; as well as engagements in the Scaling Up Nutrition (SUN) network and the Global Alliance for Improved Nutrition (GAIN). In terms of Ireland's ability to mobilise additional private finance, the government is currently only tracking the leveraging effects of the AADP.[6]

Ireland aims to encourage private finance and improve its development relevance, including through multilateral channels

Ireland engages with multilaterals to ensure that private finance is geared towards leaving no one behind and sustainable development in LDCs. It advocates for efforts that benefit or at a minimum do no harm to marginalised and vulnerable populations, in line with global environmental, climate and human rights standards. As such, Ireland is considered a constructive and critical member in multilateral banks and funds. Ireland scrutinises operations with regard to development outcomes, contribution to achieve the Sustainable Development Goals (SDGs), and their ability to leverage additional finance that demonstrate development impact. Good examples of this are Ireland's engagement in the discussions around the European Fund for Sustainable Development Plus and in influencing EU policy on sustainable finance.

Ireland promotes public and private investments for sustainable development. It issued its first green bond in 2018 and moved early to divest public monies – amounting to about EUR 318 million since 2018 – from fossil fuel companies and industry.[7] Dublin is a global financial centre and has been nominated as the European headquarters of the International Network of Financial Centres for Sustainability. Under the banner of the Year of Sustainable Finance, Ireland attracted investors and policy makers to share best practice and innovation around mobilising additional climate finance, for example by promoting evidence-based sustainable investing, modelling the impact on the SDGs and developing anti-greenwashing identification tools for investors. Ireland also engages the EU on sustainable finance. Based on a new strategy, Ireland monitors and seeks to influence EU policy to help to put Europe on track to meet the 2015 Paris Agreement and the 2030 Agenda.

Ireland's vibrant fin-tech sector could provide new opportunities for development co-operation. For example, the industry provides cost-saving solutions for a wide range of companies in Ireland that could help to reduce the costs of banking transfers and remittances.[8]

Ireland also pushes for development relevance in multilateral discussions on global trade. Ireland actively supports the participation of LDCs in World Trade Organization trade negotiations, weighs in on partner countries' needs in multilateral trade policy and international labour law discussions, and considers mandatory human rights due diligence as a requirement for all state-run and supported companies including in Ireland's partner countries. It also uses ODA to support programmes such as TradeMark East Africa that aim to reduce trade barriers and increase business competitiveness. But action on some of these efforts are perceived as slow by external stakeholders, for example on operationalising the human rights due diligence recommendation from 2017. Ireland's business presence in Ireland's partner countries (including Enterprise Ireland offices) and Irish foreign direct investment in relevant value chains also remain marginal.

A new whole-of-government approach provides momentum to help to strengthen tax systems and domestic resource mobilisation in partner countries

A Better World **commits Ireland to strengthening domestic resource mobilisation (DRM) through effective partnerships**. DRM activities remain limited and ODA allocations are small,[9] but Ireland aims to double funding to DRM partners by 2020 and to systematically increase its support to strengthening DRM capabilities and tax systems in partner countries. These are to be accomplished in part through planned increases in Ireland's contributions to the Addis Tax Initiative, the OECD Tax for Development effort and the African Tax Administration Forum. Ireland also provides training for tax authorities in partner countries.

Ireland recently launched a whole-of-government initiative to pool its experience in mobilising domestic resources. This initiative is geared towards supporting partner countries' tax administrations and enhancing their capacity for sustainable DRM. A cross-government DRM group – involving the Office of the Revenue Commissioners, the Department of Finance and the Department of Foreign Affairs and Trade – is supporting the co-ordination, assessment, and set-up of bilateral and multilateral agreements and sharing of information. The offers to partner countries are demand-driven and tailored to partners' needs, assessed with innovative diagnostic tools, and geared to complementing ongoing reform efforts. Building on its own expertise and interests, Ireland can add the most value by ensuring that its DRM advice and services are focused on building capacity to ensure that increased revenue supports all parts of populations, in particular those furthest behind. Examples of Ireland's efforts in this direction include its focus on the differential impact on women and men of tax reforms and the training that Ireland provides for dispute resolution and treaty negotiations. Ireland can also leverage its engagement with international financial institutions on tax matters and the global tax architecture and with regional and global DRM actors to share its experience in this area more systematically and foster peer learning.

References

Department of Finance, Ireland (2019), *Ireland for Finance: The Strategy for the Development of Ireland's International Financial Services Sector to 2025*, https://assets.gov.ie/24482/278893738e764db79c43eada83c030e3.pdf.   [5]

Joint Committee on Foreign Affairs and Trade, A. (2018), *Review of the Irish Aid Programme*, Houses of the Oireachtas, Dublin, https://data.oireachtas.ie/ie/oireachtas/committee/dail/32/joint_committee_on_foreign_affairs_and_trade_and_defence/reports/2018/2018-02-22_report-review-of-the-irish-aid-programme_en.pdf (accessed on 6 November 2019).   [2]

OECD (2019), *Creditor Reporting System (database)*, https://stats.oecd.org/Index.aspx?DataSetCode=crs1.   [1]

OECD DAC (2019), *DAC Statistical Reporting Issues in 2018 on Flows in 2017*, OECD Publishing, Paris.   [3]

World Bank (2019), *Migration and Remittances Data (database)*, https://www.worldbank.org/en/topic/migrationremittancesdiasporaissues/brief/migration-remittances-data (accessed on 8 November 2019).   [4]

Notes

[1] Almost one third of the recent increase in ODA volumes relates to in-donor refugee costs that Ireland started reporting in 2017, based on the new guidelines issued by the OECD DAC and the methodology that Ireland put in place with the assistance of the OECD.

[2] Exceptions concern scholarship programmes for study in Ireland as well as the Africa Agri-Food development programme that is limited to Irish companies. Alternatively, Ireland could open up its private sector partnerships to companies based outside of Ireland, as many DAC members do.

[3] All DAC countries combined provided 28.4% of their total ODA as multilateral ODA in 2018 (grant equivalent basis and according to preliminary data).

[4] All DAC countries combined provided 21.4% of their bilateral ODA through multilateral organisations in 2017 (flow basis).

[5] The programme has grown in scope, is now available in 16 African countries and, to date, has leveraged EUR 6.4 million of additional private finance. To expand the programme, Ireland aims to push into sectors such as fintech, where Ireland has expertise, and to connect it to other initiatives such as the European Commission's Taskforce for Rural Africa. Ireland also aims to place emphasis on female entrepreneurship and climate innovation in the current round of financing.

[6] Going forward, the new private sector strategy may be used to identify Irish activities and partnerships that mobilise additional private finance and where mobilisation amounts can be measured, including in the multilateral space. These also may include activities related to the Sustainable Development Goals, such as climate action.

[7] Ireland has EUR 4.2 trillion worth of assets under administration; 75% of the 430 firms in the sector are foreign-owned (Department of Finance, Ireland, 2019[5]).

[8] Remittances from Ireland accounted for 0.4% of Irish gross domestic product in 2018, or USD 1.7 billion. See (World Bank, 2019[4]) at https://www.worldbank.org/en/topic/migrationremittancesdiasporaissues/brief/migration-remittances-data.

[9] ODA to DRM amounted to USD 451 000 in 2017; the 2013-15 annual average was USD 288 000.

4 Ireland's structure and systems

This chapter considers whether Ireland's institutional arrangements support its development co-operation objectives. It focuses on the system as a whole and assesses whether Ireland has the necessary capabilities in place to deliver its development co-operation effectively and to contribute to sustainable development.

The chapter looks at authority, mandate and co-ordination to assess whether responsibility for development co-operation is clearly defined. It further explores whether the system is well co-ordinated and led with clear, complementary mandates as part of a whole-of-government approach at headquarters and in partner countries. Focusing on systems the chapter further evaluates whether Ireland has clear and relevant processes and mechanisms in place. Finally, it looks at capacity across Ireland's development co-operation system – in particular whether Ireland has the necessary skills and knowledge where needed, to manage and deliver its development co-operation – and at the effectiveness of its human resources management system.

In brief

The Department of Foreign Affairs and Trade (DFAT) leads Ireland's development co-operation and intends to further strengthen a whole-of-government approach. Numerous good practices of collaboration are already in place, and a revamped interdepartmental committee on development co-operation will discuss priorities, share experiences and monitor progress towards delivery of *A Better World*. Co-ordination within DFAT works well but in many ways relies on informal contacts, a practice that may not be sustainable if ODA is scaled up.

A new Standard Approach to Grant Management has clarified decision making by establishing a clear delegation of authority and improved risk management. Risk management responsibilities and processes are clear, and internal and external controls are effective. Ireland focuses on financial risk, with less of a focus on strategic and operational risks. It is taking steps to respond to the new DAC recommendation on preventing sexual exploitation and abuse. There is also potential to further step up anti-corruption work beyond programme management. Ireland is willing to take risks, operating mostly in challenging contexts, and promotes innovation on the ground.

Growth in the ODA budget will require further reflection on effective quality assurance and investment in information technology (IT) and e-based processes. Human resources challenges put Ireland's development co-operation system under strain. Low levels of staffing and high levels of turnover affect the level and quality of engagement. Ireland does not yet have clarity on how to match skills and jobs; it has three different staff categories but uses them interchangeably. Delivery against the objectives of *A Better World* will require more expertise under the relevant priorities, and access to training is not systematic. Implementation of the DFAT human resources strategic action plan and the planned management review are opportunities to address these important challenges. DFAT has made good progress on gender equality in staffing. Local staff are highly valued as a critical element of Irish development co-operation and enjoy good working conditions.

DFAT leads Ireland's development co-operation and intends to further strengthen a whole-of-government approach

Ireland is committed to a whole-of-government approach to development co-operation under the clear leadership of the Department of Foreign Affairs and Trade (DFAT). The national Sustainable Development Goal (SDG) implementation plan assigns lead Government Departments for each of the 169 SDG targets (Government of Ireland, 2018[1]). DFAT is the lead for virtually all development co-operation-related activities, but the plan also makes clear that other departments have a role to play. *A Better World* uses the same approach, identifying the departments DFAT will co-operate with in the pursuit of Ireland's objectives (Government of Ireland, 2019[2]). In practice, DFAT directly manages 65% of the total official development assistance (ODA) and oversees engagement with the European Union, which accounts for an additional 26% of Ireland's ODA (in 2018). Other departments mainly oversee the multilateral engagement with development banks (Department of Finance) and special mandate institutions, notably of the United Nations system.

There are numerous good practices involving collaboration across the government. DFAT works closely with the Department of Finance through secondments, regular consultation and the new initiative on domestic resource mobilisation (Chapter 3). With the Department of Agriculture, Food and the Marine, DFAT has long-standing co-operation under the Africa Agri-food Development Programme (AADP) and regarding Rome-based multilateral agencies. A memorandum of understanding with the Health Service Executive (HSE) guides the HSE's technical assistance in partner countries. Together with the Departments of Defence and of Justice and Equality, DFAT implements the National Plan on Women, Peace and Security (Chapter 1). Regular co-ordination meetings are held across the government on issues such as trade, peacekeeping and human rights. DFAT also plays an active role in the Inter-Departmental Working Group on the SDGs. The move towards action by the government of Ireland is increasingly visible in policies and publications.

Ireland is determined to take advantage of the full potential for cross-government co-operation. In *A Better World*, Ireland commits to "develop strategies for deepening co-ordination across Government to deliver on our policy priorities". As a first, important step, the government will expand the role of the inter-departmental committee (IDC) on development co-operation. The IDC will thus cover the Irish ODA budget and not only the ODA through DFAT, and would meet more frequently to discuss each department's priorities, monitor progress towards delivery of *A Better World* and share experiences (Department of Foreign Affairs and Trade, Ireland, 2019[3]). This could help to share quality standards and approaches developed by DFAT and allow line departments to integrate their technical expertise. The planned multilateral framework (Chapter 2) is an opportunity to guide a whole-of-government approach, in particular where multiple departments engage, notably on food, environment and climate, health and finance.

Bilateral actions of other departments are not part of the whole-of-mission country strategy approach. This is understandable, considering their very limited engagement. At the same time, ad hoc interventions are less likely to make a sustainable contribution to development in the partner country. There is thus a need to reflect if Ireland should bring in the expertise of line departments as part of its co-operation at country level and if so, how.

Co-ordination within DFAT works well but relies on informal contacts, a practice that may not be sustainable if ODA is scaled up

Co-ordination within DFAT works generally well at all levels. Ireland has successfully moved forward the integration of development co-operation into DFAT. The newly named Development Cooperation and Africa Division (DCAD) is now also responsible for political relations with Africa. Previously split administrative and support units (e.g. evaluation and audit, and communications) now service the entire department. While these units are located outside DCAD, their collaboration with DCAD is generally good. Building on clearly assigned responsibilities, the headquarters and missions collaborate well, as seen in Ethiopia (Annex C). As a good practice, DFAT also enables the exchange between missions so that technical expertise in one mission can benefit another (Annex C). Expanding co-operation beyond Africa (e.g. to small island developing states, Latin America and Caribbean, and the Middle East) will require clarifying the link between regional units and DCAD.[1] The planned management review is an opportunity to identify possible friction points and solutions.

However, co-ordination relies in many ways on informal contacts, a practice that may not be sustainable if ODA is scaled up. In the Irish aid system, co-ordination relies on personal acquaintance and knowing whom to talk to (often summarised as "We all know each other"). While this works reasonably well, limits to this approach are evident now and will likely multiply as the ODA budget increases. The split between Dublin and Limerick offices adds a further challenge to exchange with Dublin-based stakeholders outside DFAT as well as within DFAT units, as not all staff are located with their managers. The still-limited use of e-based processes and IT infrastructure further impedes co-ordination, although investments are being made in these, as is discussed elsewhere. High turnover makes it more challenging to know whom to talk to. Moreover, local staff in embassies are not necessarily familiar with colleagues elsewhere. Informal contacts also rely on the good will of all involved. More structured and systematic co-ordination could help to address these challenges, especially in a growing system.

Systems

A new Standard Approach to Grant Management has clarified decision making and improved risk management

Mechanisms for decision making are clear and delegation of authority meaningful. Units are responsible for the design of strategies and policies,[2] which are then reviewed and approved at management level. For individual grants, the 2017 Standard Approach to Grant Management (SAGM) clearly sets out responsibilities and processes. For programme approval, heads of embassies and heads of units have delegated authority up to EUR 3.0 million (multi-year programmes) or EUR 1.5 million (single year programmes), unless the risk warrants escalation to a higher level of authority. This provides meaningful delegation of authority by covering a large range of Ireland's engagement. Levels could be reconsidered if the ODA budget grows substantially, also taking into consideration the relatively higher workload of many small projects.

Risk management responsibilities and processes are clear. The 2014 risk management policy established responsibilities across all hierarchical levels and identified the range of risks Ireland would need to manage.[3] An internal analysis also issued in 2014 identified as a main weakness the divergent practices of formalisation and documentation (Evaluation and Audit Unit, DFAT, 2014[4]). By providing detailed guidance, the SAGM remedied this challenge. Grant managers systematically assess risks and reflect mitigating measures in appraisal, contracting, monitoring and internal reporting. Risk registers exist at all levels and are regularly discussed and updated. The obligation to document risks and actions taken ensures that line managers also engage in risk management, supported by a designated chief risk officer at senior management level.

Internal and external controls are effective. A recent external review confirmed the effectiveness of the internal audit function, ensured by the Evaluation and Audit Unit and internal auditors in embassies. The Comptroller and Auditor General regularly assess internal controls. In addition, the Audit Committee provides independent advice to the Accounting Officer (Secretary General) on the suitability and robustness of internal controls and procedures. Their findings are positive, and DFAT has ensured follow-up to main recommendations.[4]

Ireland pays significant attention to the management of financial risk. The SAGM requires a detailed analysis of partner capacity and funding flows, including guidance on whether implementing partners have the capacity for onward granting. A counter-fraud policy, legislation and procedures on protected disclosure, and information on whistleblowing complement the SAGM. Importantly, zero tolerance of fraud does not mean zero risk for Ireland, but rather is meant to encourage systematic reporting and follow-up. These can include investigations and, where the situation requires, suspension of payments or cancellation of contracts. Ireland regularly publishes information with regard to incidents of suspected fraud.

There is potential to further step up anti-corruption work. Embassies develop corruption profiles as part of their country strategies. These profiles are an opportunity to look beyond mismanagement of funds and assess how Ireland can contribute to the fight against corruption in a given country context. Integrating training on anti-corruption into risk management training and developing a code of conduct could help to guide staff on problems and dilemmas in everyday work situations and strengthen awareness and understanding of risks. This could also include greater clarity on what should be considered cases of suspected fraud and which of these should be reported to headquarters and how (Annex C).

Ireland could improve guidance on strategic and some operational risks. The SAGM and standard templates use yes-or-no questions to prompt grant managers to confirm that the programme is sensitive to environmental effects, good governance requirements or conflict or that the organisation has appropriate child protection measures in place.[5] Ireland does not have a specific safeguarding policy, but engages with implementing partners to assess their approach to safeguards.[6] However, in the absence of (updated) guidance on relevant issues, grant managers and implementing organisations might not always be able to ascertain if they have made appropriate provision in response to such risks.

Specifically with regard to preventing sexual exploitation, abuse and harassment (PSEAH), Ireland is taking concrete steps to follow up on the new DAC recommendation. Following its co-leadership in facilitating the new DAC recommendation, it has started developing a specific safeguards policy on PSEAH[7] that will codify existing practice and complement internal disciplinary standards. As Ireland operates in challenging contexts, it will be particularly important to consider which oversight mechanisms and incentives will be introduced to ensure that implementing partners and their subcontractors train their staff, self-report, investigate and respond to all cases using a survivor-centred approach. This will require raising awareness among staff and implementing partners about their obligations in relation to the DAC recommendation. Dóchas, the umbrella organisation of Irish civil society organisations (CSOs), has already developed a safeguarding code that provides guidance on key issues (Dóchas, 2019[5]).

Ireland does not shy away from taking risks. The SAGM refers to actions "with a minimum of risk", but this does not mean risk avoidance. Ireland, in fact, is willing to take risks as it is operating mostly in challenging contexts. The 2014 risk management policy is very clear that DFAT must take risks to reach its objectives. DFAT could clarify its risk appetite using its existing tools, which could help to balance risks within and across its portfolio and in particular when considering Ireland's objective to reach the furthest behind first.

Ireland promotes innovation on the ground. As a small donor with good influence in sector dialogue, Ireland strategically supports pilots to generate evidence for discussions with the partner government and other donors (Annex C). As a first mover, Ireland is able to rapidly react to changes in context and thereby create momentum for other donors to follow suit. Through its strategic partnerships, Ireland provides great flexibility to civil society partners to enable innovation and includes innovation as one of its funding criteria. Ireland does not have centralised mechanisms for innovation.[8] Investments in horizontal learning could spur replication of successful innovation within the Irish development co-operation system.

Growth in the ODA budget will require further reflection on effective quality assurance and investment in IT and e-based processes

As its development co-operation programme grows, Ireland could reconsider whether it strikes the balance on quality assurance well. In the development of mission strategies, Ireland mobilises extensive expertise and has a compulsory internal and external quality assurance in place. For individual project proposals, responsibility for quality assurance lies with the grant manager. While technical experts are often involved in practice, the SAGM does not require grant managers to draw on their expertise for the specific sector, region or cross-cutting issues. This contrasts with compulsory controls for financial matters and with strategic funding to CSOs, which involves two appraisers reviewing submissions independently from one another in addition to expert review. At the same time and given its staffing constraints, Ireland would not have the capacity to backstop every programme.[9] When arbitrating this trade-off, Ireland could consider flexible approaches such as making spot checks, imposing greater scrutiny for flagship or pilot programmes, and drawing on evaluation findings to identify issues that require greater attention. This could be complemented by a more complete body of guidance (Chapter 2) to inform grant managers of more recent international good practice and learning in their sector.

DFAT has recognised the need for more e-based processes and investment in IT infrastructure. However, it will take some years to see significant change, as an e-based system to manage grants is currently being piloted outside DCAD,[10] and upgrades to the IT system can only be effected for the entire department. For the moment, staff are required to maintain the paper file on grants as evidence. Well-managed investments[11] are likely to increase efficiency, improve data management, facilitate knowledge exchange between missions and headquarters, and promote institutional learning. Table 4.1 presents an assessment of Ireland's development co-operation systems, based on documentation and information provided to OECD by the government of Ireland.

Table 4.1. Assessment of Ireland's development co-operation systems

	Yes	Progress	No	Comment
Clear and transparent processes and procedures are in place to make decisions on:				
• Programming	●			▲ Clear responsibilities and meaningful delegation of authority to units and embassies
• Policies (Chapter 2)	●			
• Partnerships (Chapters 2 and 5)	●			▲ Clear criteria for programmes ● Requiring information on considered alternatives for direct awards and guidance for selection between different types of partners could be useful
Systems are in place to assure the quality of development co-operation, including:				
• Audit	●			▲ Satisfactory internal audit function and external controls.
• Mainstreaming cross-cutting issues (Chapter 2)		●		● Strong involvement for country strategies, (outdated) guidance for gender equality and environment in place, and SAGM not clear on involvement of experts.
Systems support the member to implement its policies and commitments in a fair and efficient way:				
• Procurement, contracting, agreement-making	●			▲ Clear guidance and templates: implementing partners must respect transparency and fairness in procurement, and Ireland assesses their capacity. ● Direct awards in country can lead to inefficiencies. No reporting on awarded contracts.
Adequate and relevant systems and processes to assess and adapt to risks, including:				
• Strategic, reputational, programming, security	●			▲ Strong systems and guidance in place, regular risk monitoring and mitigation measures. ● Absence of broader safeguards policies with regard to social or environmental aspects.
• Corruption	●			▲ Strong attention on financial risk in grant management. ● The corruption risk assessment could go beyond financials risks; country profiles are an opportunity to understand corruption in a wider country context.
• Sexual exploitation, abuse and harassment		●		▲ PSEAH covered by disciplinary standards and DFAT's child safeguarding policy and explicitly included in codes of conduct ● No specific guidance beyond child protection in place yet, but a safeguarding policy currently being developed.
Innovation and adaptation:				
• The leadership and internal system promote a culture of experimentation and adaptability to changes in the development landscape	●			▲ Culture of engaging in challenging contexts and reacting rapidly to changes in context.
• Capabilities exist to introduce, encourage, measure and scale up innovation in development co-operation.		●		▲ Pilots to engage donors; encouragement of CSOs through programme grants. ● No systematic approach to measure and scale up innovation.

Note: The green triangles refer to good practice; orange circles point to areas where progress is being made but more could be done.
Source: Developed by the OECD Secretariat following the structure of the DAC Peer Review Reference Guide and based on documentation and information provided by the Irish government.

Capabilities throughout the system

Insufficient staffing and human resources challenges put the development co-operation system under strain

Low levels of staffing create significant challenges for Ireland. Through a 2018 internal study, DCAD identified that HQ staff numbers declined 25% over the previous ten years (DFAT Evaluation and Audit Unit, 2018[6]). Recent hires have restored staffing to 2012 levels, but the level of funding in constant terms is already significantly higher in 2018 than it was 2012.[12] In *A Better World*, Ireland explicitly acknowledges that growing the ODA budget requires investment in capacity. Indeed, low staffing is a risk for partner engagement and grant management. Moreover, relying on the very high intrinsic motivation of staff increases risks for their well-being. DCAD also continues to depend on junior professional interns as temporary replacements for core staff. Despite the challenges, Ireland has not yet developed a medium-term staff plan as the 2014 peer review recommended.

Staff and partners alike express concern at high levels of turnover, which affect the level and quality of engagement. The percentage of staff who are in their current position less than two years is 82%, whereas a three to four-year rotation cycle should lead to a ratio of between 50% and 67%. One-day inductions are systematic, but only for new hires and limited to providing information on administrative matters and introducing colleagues. Staff are required to complete a handover note, and the SAGM makes settling in easier, but further investment may be required in on-boarding of staff who are assuming new positions. This would be particularly important in the case of staff without a development background who start working in DCAD.

Ireland does not yet have clarity on how to match skills and jobs. Three types of staff are recruited to DFAT in Ireland: diplomats (who must rotate), generalists (who may rotate) and development specialists (who must rotate among development positions). While this division suggests that development specialists fill all posts that are related to development co-operation, the practice at headquarters is quite different. Diplomats, generalists and development specialists all work in DCAD, including in identical functions. At higher levels, development specialists have also successfully been promoted into diplomatic positions outside DCAD or become ambassadors. As staff have a strong sense of the difference between categories, greater clarity on each category's purpose could contribute to greater staff cohesion. The forthcoming management review offers an opportunity for this to be addressed. DFAT management, which seeks to broaden skillsets through greater mobility across functions, has aligned the pay scales of development specialists and civil service grades, facilitating mobility and enhancing opportunities. This could significantly enhance skillsets that are relevant for development on issues such as diplomacy, conflict prevention, trade and collaboration with line ministries. However, DFAT has not yet clarified how it intends to take advantage of a specific background in development, or whether it requires deep technical expertise in house on particular issues.

If Ireland wants to deliver against the objectives of *A Better World*, it will require more dedicated expertise for its priorities. At present, only one person at DFAT headquarters leads on each of the areas of gender, climate, food, governance and the private sector. While humanitarian assistance is covered by a distinct unit, its staff mostly focus on programme management. Dedicated staff for its priorities would allow Ireland to deepen its expertise, learn across the system, provide targeted advice to staff and engage partners more effectively.

Access to training is not systematic. Ireland regularly provides training on administrative topics. It also reached some staff through a specific training on gender equality but has not invested in systematic training on other issues. Moreover, staff do not always take advantage of training due to time constraints, leading to significant unmet training needs[13] (Government of Ireland, 2019[7]).

DFAT has made good progress on gender equality in leadership. Across development specialist grades, there are slightly more women than men, including in senior management and postings abroad. In the entire department, many more positions are filled by women than men. However, fewer women than men in total are posted abroad. Through its gender and diversity committee DFAT is looking at the reasons for this disparity. There are clear incentives such as subsequent cross-postings for taking on posts in challenging locations. However, support for expatriate spouses is still limited.[14] DFAT has recognised it can do more to promote diversity in staffing and adopted a specific action plan to support diversity and equality in 2018.

Local staff are highly valued as a critical element of Irish development co-operation. Local staff make up 25% of the total co-operation workforce and manage grants, inform political dialogue, bring technical expertise and local knowledge, and hold institutional memory. As seen in Ethiopia, they are empowered to represent Ireland, and partners value their quality engagement (Annex C).

Working conditions for local staff are good, with potential for better consultation at headquarters level. As seen in Ethiopia, satisfaction with working conditions, integration and a sense of being appreciated are strong factors supporting retention. Contracts apply the more beneficial clauses of either Irish or local law, overtime work is compensated, and salaries are increased regularly in line with agreed pay scales and procedures. Ireland also invests in the skills development of local staff, enabling training opportunities (including abroad) identified through the annual performance management process. Nevertheless, opportunities for career progression are limited[15] and Ireland has limited flexibility on salary for particularly competitive posts (e.g. regional experts). Some staff therefore take up opportunities to grow elsewhere. As a good practice, the Irish Embassy in Ethiopia solicited and reflected comments from local staff on staff administration. DFAT headquarters set up a local staff helpdesk in 2018 and holds an annual meeting of local heads of administration. It could reflect how it gives local staff an opportunity to be heard on human resources policies that affect them, for instance by consulting local staff representatives.

Implementing the DFAT human resources strategic action plan and the management review present an opportunity to address challenges. DFAT would greatly benefit from identifying the skills, expertise and staffing levels needed to implement *A Better World* and establishing a timeline for staff to be hired, integrated and systematically trained. The Human Resources Strategic Action Plan 2019-2022 sets out all the important issues: workforce planning, skills needs assessments, enhancing retention in areas of turnover, gender and diversity, and better training for all staff. The forthcoming management review is an ideal opportunity to address constraints, engage with staff and ultimately ensure a structure that is fit for purpose to deliver on *A Better World*.

References

Department of Foreign Affairs and Trade, Ireland (2019), *Inter-Departmental Committee on Development Co-operation: Terms of Reference (draft)*, Government of Ireland, Dublin, http://unpublished. [3]

DFAT Evaluation and Audit Unit (2018), *Assessment of Staff Resourcing for Partner Management in the Development Cooperation Division: Executive Summary*. [6]

Dóchas (2019), *Dóchas Safeguarding Code*, Irish Association of Non-Government Organisations (Dóchas), Dublin, https://dochas.ie/sites/default/files/Dochas_Safeguarding_Code.pdf. [5]

Evaluation and Audit Unit, DFAT (2014), *Assessment of Internal Control and Risk Management Systems in Key Partner Countries: Synthesis Report*. [4]

Government of Australia (2019), *Preventing Sexual Exploitation, Abuse and Harassment Policy*, [8]
Department of Trade and Foreign Affairs, Canberra, https://dfat.gov.au/international-relations/themes/preventing-sexual-exploitation-abuse-and-harassment/Documents/pseah-policy.pdf.

Government of Ireland (2019), *A Better World: Ireland's Policy for International Development*, [2]
https://www.irishaid.ie/media/irishaid/aboutus/abetterworldirelandspolicyforinternationaldevelopment/A-Better-World-Irelands-Policy-for-International-Development.pdf.

Government of Ireland (2019), *DAC Peer Review 2020: Memorandum of Ireland*. [7]

Government of Ireland (2018), *The Sustainable Development Goals National Implementation Plan 2018-2020*, https://www.dccae.gov.ie/documents/DCCAE-National-Implement-Plan.pdf. [1]

USAID (2018), *USAID's Policy Against Sexual Exploitation and Abuse (webpage)*, [9]
https://www.usaid.gov/PreventingSexualMisconduct/fact-sheets/usaid-policy-against-sexual-exploitation-and-abuse.

Notes

[1] For instance, the Civil Society Unit manages Ireland's development co-operation with the West Bank and Gaza Strip and Viet Nam, while partnerships with other partner countries are covered by the Africa Unit and other divisions cover relations with the Middle East and Asia.

[2] The Standard Approach & Process Guide to Mission Strategy Planning clearly sets out the process for embassies (Chapter 2).

[3] These include strategic, operational, financial and reputational risks.

[4] The Audit Committee suggested to include audit report recommendations that were not followed-up upon in the risk register (started in 2017) and to provide a timeline for follow-up as well as to enhance the fraud register to identify trends or systemic issues (increased capacity of the Evaluation and Audit Unit will enable better follow-up). The Comptroller and Auditor General recommended including mitigating measures in grant agreements (leading to an update of the SAGM) and publishing the fraud register (started in 2018).

[5] The sample Memorandum of Understanding attached to the SAGM includes provisions on contributing towards the promotion and protection of the environment (although it does not mention environmental impact assessments), on promoting gender equality, and on carrying out a gender analysis as part of the project preparation.

[6] This includes explicit safeguards requirements in DFAT headquarters funding lines for civil society organisations (CSOs); specific contractual requirements for child protection; engagement with Irish CSOs on their approach to safeguarding (a Dóchas Working Group currently works on safeguarding); and engagement with multilateral organisations.

[7] Australia recently published a Preventing Sexual Exploitation, Abuse and Harassment Policy (Government of Australia, 2019[8]). The United States Agency for International Development also has a specific policy against sexual exploitation and abuse (USAID, 2018[9]).

[8] The Africa Strategy and Innovation Fund is not a specific innovation tool, but rather serves as a budget line for Ireland's engagement with regional organisations and countries of secondary accreditation (Chapter 2). It is explicitly not designed for activities that could be part of any embassy budget and thus scaled up by Ireland itself.

[9] This is also why the SAGM prompts grant managers to indicate the estimated workload for colleagues who would support grant implementation, as was recommended in the 2014 peer review.

[10] The reason the system is piloted outside DCAD is to test it first in a context of fewer and less complex grants.

[11] Lessons from other donors' experience suggests a need for close management to avoid significant delays and cost increases.

[12] The 2018 funding level is USD 891 million compared to USD 767 million in 2012.

[13] Ireland estimates that 60-70% of training needs are met (Government of Ireland, 2019[7]).

[14] This support could include pre-departure training that covers particular challenges faced by expatriate spouses, support for activities where paid employment is not feasible, and the conclusion of agreements with host states or co-operation with other sending states.

[15] As some DAC members, Ireland could explore offering short-term or longer-term opportunities for local staff in DFAT headquarters or other embassies.

5 Ireland's delivery modalities and partnerships

This chapter looks at the principles that guide Ireland's partnership approach across its development portfolio and how Ireland uses its financial, diplomatic and technical resources in its global engagement and in partner countries. It assesses whether the approach and principles are consistent with Ireland's development co-operation policy and international commitments on development effectiveness: ownership of development priorities by developing countries; a focus on results; inclusive development partnerships; and transparency and mutual accountability.

The chapter first considers Ireland's approach to partnerships for development co-operation with a range of actors, assessing whether they embody the development effectiveness principles. It then explores whether Ireland's work in partner countries is in keeping with its domestic and international commitments to, and principles of, effective development co-operation.

In brief

Its long-lasting commitment to engagement in partnerships is the trademark of Ireland's development co-operation. This partnership approach also provides the backdrop for realising *A Better World*. Ireland's partnerships with civil society are particularly strong and are characterised by mutual trust, quality funding based on clear criteria and an open culture for substantive, regular dialogue.

Known for its strong commitment to multilateralism, Ireland is also considered a reliable partner to multilateral organisations. Building on good funding practices, Ireland seeks to intensify strategic dialogue with its multilateral partners. For some humanitarian partners, it has already moved away from committing funding on a yearly basis. Ireland is much appreciated for its constructive engagement in boards and strategy development.

The ambition of *A Better World* to partner with research organisations and the private sector will require more substantial engagement that recognises the need to rebuild and expand its research partnerships and to intensify dialogue that contributes to the articulation of Ireland's private sector engagement strategy.

Ireland is also actively engaging at the country level. It uses joint approaches, takes a proactive role in donor co-ordination and political dialogue to make its voice heard and is making efforts to improve the quality of its aid information. Ireland continues to champion development effectiveness but has room for improvement in the application of the effectiveness principles across its modalities and partnerships. For instance, Ireland could make progress on ownership, alignment and the use of country systems, and there is scope to strengthen its medium-term predictability for the benefit of its partner countries.

Ireland's partnership approach provides the backdrop for realising A Better World

Ireland's long-standing commitment to engaging in partnerships is the trademark of its development co-operation. A trusted and energetic partner, Ireland is known and appreciated for the long-term and principled support it provides, often making the extra effort to ensure partnerships deliver beyond expectation and in ways that respond effectively in some of the most challenging and fast-changing environments. *A Better World* is keeping a focus on directing ODA to partnerships, in particular those that directly help people living in difficult contexts. The new policy also places emphasis on innovative partnership opportunities that maximise Ireland's footprint and the impact of its development interventions in line with the needs of its partner countries. Ireland strives to make all its partnerships effective and, like other development partners, has advocated for recognition of such efforts in the current monitoring through the Global Partnership for Effective Development Co-operation (GPEDC).

Ireland promotes multi-stakeholder dialogue. Specific platforms on agriculture, health, development education and violence against women that bring together government, civil society, academia and the private sector foster regular exchange and co-ordination. Ireland's leadership role as chair of the Task Team on CSO Development Effectiveness and Enabling Environment is an illustration of the commitment to multi-stakeholder dialogue, in this instance to advance effective civil society participation in development processes. While Ireland funds many partners that participate in these types of dialogue structures and provides ad hoc support for specific activities or initiatives, it does not have instruments that could provide systematic and longer-term funding for joint initiatives that could emerge through these platforms.

Quality funding and dialogue distinguish Ireland's civil society partnerships

Partnerships with Irish and local civil society organisations (CSOs) are characterised by mutual trust and an open culture of substantive, regular dialogue. Ireland engages closely with its CSOs on all aspects of its co-operation, often through informal dialogue that at times can be resource-intensive. Umbrella organisations not only help Irish CSOs join forces in advocacy, but also drive quality through knowledge exchange and code of conducts. Among these are Dóchas for development non-governmental organisations (NGOs) including faith-based organisations; Comhlámh for volunteering agencies; and the Irish Development Education Association for development education. Irish CSOs welcome the government's progressive approach to promoting civic space and consider the government a potent ally in global policy debates.

Ireland provides its funding to CSOs based on clear criteria, focusing on where needs are greatest and on engaging with a wide range of partners in predictable and flexible ways and through appropriate channels. These make Ireland an indispensable partner and role model for civil society partnerships (Box 5.1). At the same time, Ireland has strengthened its due diligence and risk management processes related to all its partnerships (Chapter 4). This has raised the overall quality standards. However, some CSOs are concerned about what they perceive as a shift away from Ireland's partnership model to a contractual relationship for implementation, and an associated high administrative burden, particularly for smaller organisations. Ireland provides quality and predictable funding through annual disbursements, early on in the implementation cycle, and is considered to be flexible in terms of adjusting in-year, also to avoid challenges arising from the obligation for partners to spend resources within the calendar year in which they have been allocated.

> ### Box 5.1. The quality of funding to civil society organisations
>
> Ireland has consistently ranked among the DAC donors with the highest percentage of bilateral official development assistance (ODA) channelled to and through civil society. With most of its bilateral ODA allocated to CSOs as core contributions (Chapter 3), Ireland places great emphasis on supporting CSOs as independent development actors. Allocations to and through CSOs were also safeguarded during the financial crisis and its aftermath. In 2017-18, CSOs for the first time also received funding under a joint humanitarian and programme grant arrangement.
>
> DFAT selects Irish CSO partners for funding based on a competitive and rigorous screening process. The CSO programme grant assesses CSO proposals based on clearly identified criteria. Ireland requires co-funding from all its civil society partners. Missionary Orders that are members of Misean Cara contribute at least 25% of the total cost of projects in cash or in kind. Diplomatic missions also have the ability to provide direct support to partners that are pre-identified and vetted for their organisational capacity to deliver. Ireland provides predictable funding where appropriate through multi-year agreements. For example, contributions to 13 Irish NGOs in 2017 are committed for up to 5 years, with grants ranging from EUR 500 000 up to EUR 20 million, totalling an estimated EUR 320 million (2017-2021) and partners having great flexibility in the use of their funding. Agreements of up to 3 years are now common for humanitarian assistance (Chapter 7).
>
> Ireland makes good use of joint approaches with other development partners in funding CSOs, including for example pooled funds that reduce partners' reporting burden and are considered largely more effective than individual programmes. As became evident in the field visit in Ethiopia, there is an impressive diversity of such efforts, in particular through the Civil Society Support Programme and the Ethiopia Social Accountability Programme (Annex C).

Building on good funding practices, Ireland seeks to intensify strategic dialogue with multilaterals

Ireland is considered a reliable partner by multilateral organisations and is known for its strong commitment to multilateralism. This is reflected in the large share of its ODA going to core contributions, for which it is appreciated. Over 50% of Ireland's earmarked contributions to the United Nations (UN) in 2017 were provided through UN interagency pooled funds. This is the highest share of any UN member country and is politically important in the context of the UN reform (Dag Hammarskjöld Foundation/UN, 2019[1]).

Ireland is increasingly moving towards multi-annual funding for its multilateral partners. Funding to multilaterals is part of long-lasting partnerships with the respective institutions, though many partners do not have a framework (or multi-year) agreement or a memorandum of understanding with Ireland. As Ireland has already moved to multi-annual funding for some multilaterals that are focused on humanitarian assistance, it could consider doing the same for all multilaterals. Ireland is appreciated for making its payments on time, with some partners reporting slight delays, and for its high degree of flexibility in using and reprogramming funds. Ireland is also valued as a donor with appropriate reporting requirements and limited transaction costs. One exception is the management burden that can arise in the context of providing annual grants only, such as the negotiation of no-cost extensions for earmarked funding.

Ireland is much appreciated by its multilateral partners for its constructive engagement in boards and around strategy development, where Ireland promotes its own policy priorities in coherent and focused ways. It is known for making a point of ensuring that poverty orientation and partner countries' needs are considered in board-level strategic programming decisions. Ireland is considered an active partner in annual strategic dialogues with priority partners that adds useful perspectives. Ireland engages actively and jointly with other donors in the context of UN reform and other reform processes, including de-linking the resident co-ordinator system in UN field offices and supporting the UN Office for the Coordination of Humanitarian Affairs to strengthen its approach to reporting on results.

Given these high standards, some multilateral partners encourage greater engagement by Ireland. This has already taken shape in the growing Irish presence in Geneva, New York and Washington, DC, including through secondments, although Ireland's presence is less in Brussels to date. A more active presence could help Ireland respond to the parliamentary request to enhance oversight over its multilateral engagement.

The ambition expressed in A Better World to partner with research organisations and the private sector will require more substantial engagement

Ireland is exploring how to rebuild and expand its research partnerships and activities to deliver cutting edge research on the priorities set out in A Better World. At present, funding is limited and often provided through EU co-financing arrangements or small grants, including through the Irish Research Council. More capacity is required to rebuild research expertise and develop long-term partnerships with a diverse set of higher education institutions, research intermediaries and learning partners to meet a diverse set of research, evidence, knowledge and learning needs. The development research landscape in the United Kingdom is attractive to universities in partner countries, and Ireland must consider how the government and Irish research institutions can strengthen their research activities to engage more systematically as part of this ecosystem or to differentiate their activities in ways that show Ireland's value added.

Ireland would benefit from stronger whole-of-government co-ordination for its private sector engagement. This could usefully build on existing partnerships between DFAT and other departments, for example with the Department of Agriculture, Food and the Marine around the AADP. DFAT could also foster more regular and open dialogue with Enterprise Ireland and other institutions such as Bord Bia (the Irish Food Board), Teagasc (the Agriculture and Food Development Authority), Sustainable Food Systems Ireland, Geoscience Ireland, and Sustainable Nation Ireland.

Dialogue with private sector partners both at headquarters and in the field can be more structured. Despite good efforts, including through the annual Africa Ireland Economic Forum, dialogue with Irish companies and potential private partners in the field remains reactive rather than proactive.[1] Consultations in preparation of Ireland's private sector strategy are helping to familiarise existing and prospective new partners with Ireland's development objectives. More regular, structured dialogue around practical challenges and opportunities can help to engage all the companies in Ireland with the necessary product mix, scale and interest and drive home the value added for Irish businesses to become actively engaged. Such dialogue would also be a first step towards a joint agenda for private sector partnerships for sustainable development in Ireland and at partner country level that brings all the different efforts under one umbrella. It would also provide a platform for discussing financing and accountability arrangements in more concerted ways.

Capacity is a prerequisite for serious private sector engagement. Strengthened technical expertise and capacity would allow DFAT to engage with other stakeholders across the government and co-ordinate the process of learning from the experience and expertise of others. Further upgrading and clustering of resources at DFAT headquarters and at mission level could also enable Ireland to seize emerging opportunities and innovative approaches to climate finance and risk insurance in Dublin as well as in hubs such as Nairobi. This could also benefit initiatives led by non-governmental organisations and the private sector to raise private finance such as the Vita Green Impact Fund and the African Agri-Growth Initiative.

Ireland uses joint approaches and takes a proactive role in donor co-ordination and political dialogue to make its voice heard

In many partner countries, Ireland is taking leadership roles in donor co-ordination, fostering critical alliances that lead to greater harmonisation among development partners and greater alignment to the needs of partners. It is widely recognised as a strategic influencer, forging consensus around key policy issues among partner country governments, development partners and other actors. Its relatively small size allows Ireland to act nimbly and to address sensitive issues at higher political levels.

The peer review team witnessed Ireland's leading role in donor co-ordination first-hand in Ethiopia. While Ireland provides only 1% of the total ODA received in Ethiopia, it plays a lead role in the Development Assistance Group, through its Executive Committee and active engagement in national and sectoral co-ordination efforts. It proactively engages in political dialogue with development partners, civil society and the government of Ethiopia, lobbying for the support it requires in its reform efforts and also addressing sensitive topics, such as the lack of civic space.

Ireland remains an advocate for mutual accountability. Building on a long history in this area, Ireland continues to support partner country governments, civil society and other stakeholders to participate in mutual assessment reviews at country and sectoral levels in meaningful ways. It helps to ensure mutuality around a shared agenda that does not place the onus for reporting on one partner and enables non-state actors to engage.

Ireland also acts as a lead donor for joint programmes, using pooled funds and other joint approaches where appropriate and cost-effective. Its engagement in Ethiopia shows the strategic roles Ireland takes in some of the major joint approaches by development partners, in particular the Productive Safety Nets Programme, which provides food and cash to millions of rural people living in poverty, including in response to economic and natural shocks. Within this challenging context, Ireland chaired the programme's Donor Working Group and led dialogue with the Ethiopian government.

About 1% of Irish total ODA is channelled through delegated co-operation (Department of Foreign Affairs and Trade, Ireland, 2017[2]), a modality that could be utilised more if ODA is being scaled up in future.

Ireland is making efforts to improve the quality of its aid information

Ireland is committed to providing access to information on the effective use of its ODA. Thanks to rigorous monitoring and oversight practices and relatively little fragmentation across ministries, Ireland is well placed to be a transparent donor. It is using annual reports and debates in the parliament to explain where and how ODA is spent. This could have greater impact if paired with an updated and interactive website that would help to foster greater citizen engagement.

Ireland can build on its achievements in aid transparency to reap benefits fully (OECD/UNDP, 2019[3]). Since the last peer review, Ireland made improvements in terms of the timeliness, completeness and accuracy of data for the OECD Creditor Reporting System, with room for improvement still around the quality of data.

Its performance in the International Aid Transparency Index has also improved on coverage, timeliness and comprehensiveness, but has deteriorated on forward-looking information. The Aid Transparency Index of Publish What You Fund (2019[4]) rates Irish Aid as "fair", placing it in the bottom quintile of performance. The organisation recommends that Ireland publish more financial and project budget data and performance-related information, and it highlights the need to better use the data Ireland publishes to promote co-ordination, effectiveness and feedback loops at partner country level. Once its information technology-based system is rolled out, Ireland could publish data on a quarterly basis and promote the use of these data across the system. This will require clear procedures alongside awareness raising and training for DFAT staff. Ireland has also significantly improved its transparency on climate finance between 2014 and 2016 (AdaptationWatch (Weikmans et al.), 2016[5]), ranking second after Germany.

Country-level engagement

Ireland continues to champion development effectiveness

In line with its foreign policy Ireland considers the effectiveness of its international development co-operation to be instrumental. *A Better World* acknowledges the importance of development effectiveness but lacks a reaffirmation of Ireland's commitment to effectiveness, which had been included in *One World, One Future*. However, the new policy document rightly observes that the principles of aid effectiveness no longer dominate, "changing the dynamics and types of policy influence at country level".

Ireland demonstrates continued leadership on development effectiveness in action at both headquarters and mission level. It has been an effectiveness advocate in its collective and multilateral engagements and actively engages in relevant global efforts, such as the GPEDC and the Multilateral Organisation Performance Assessment Network. Similarly, at country level, mission strategies signal efforts to act on the effectiveness principles, including by promoting alignment to partner country needs, monitoring and tracking results, investing in inclusive partnerships, and fostering quality assurance through oversight, value for money and risk management.

Building on a solid foundation, Ireland has room for further improvement on ownership, alignment and the use of country systems

Ireland strives to work with partner country authorities despite often challenging contexts. Reflecting a shift away from budget support, Ireland's country programmable aid dropped from 47% in 2014 to 31% of total bilateral ODA in 2018. The share of its gross bilateral ODA to the public sector is one of the lowest among DAC members, at 22% in 2017. Funding recorded in national budgets has dropped (Table 5.1) (OECD/UNDP, 2019[3]). Ireland operates in challenging environments and fragile contexts and makes efforts to deliver through the public sector where possible. The peer review team witnessed this in Ethiopia, where, despite challenges, Ireland is channelling 55% of its bilateral budget to the public sector. Ireland can continue to play a lead role in strengthening or rebuilding trust through political dialogue in its partner countries (Annex C).

Ireland is committed to taking country context as the starting point for strategic planning and programming but can improve its alignment to country priorities where appropriate. In preparing its mission strategies, Ireland consulted the government and civil society in all partner countries that reported to the GPEDC in 2018, but consulted less with private sector and other actors (OECD/UNDP, 2019[3]). Effectiveness considerations underpin the mission strategies, they are informed by national development and growth plans, and they result in a memorandum of understanding with the government. However, not in all cases are mission strategy priorities aligned to country priorities (OECD/UNDP, 2019[3]). While there may be context-specific reasons for this, Ireland strives for continued alignment at the strategic and project levels. It further should conduct joint and inclusive evaluations of mission strategies where feasible and appropriate to ensure that partner country governments continue to buy in to Ireland's bilateral development co-operation activities.

Alignment to and use of partner country results frameworks can also improve. Despite the ambition to ensure that results frameworks draw on country-level indicators, GPEDC 2018 data show that a decreasing share of Ireland's development interventions aligns to and uses country-led results frameworks to programme and design new interventions.[2] The use of country results indicators to monitor progress in the implementation of these projects also decreased (from 65% in 2016 to 55% in 2018) (OECD/UNDP, 2019[3]).

Ireland remains committed to the use of country public financial management systems and carefully studies where such engagement or re-engagement is appropriate. *A Better World* stresses its ongoing commitment to strengthening the use of country systems where appropriate. While country systems are used far less (declining from 80% in 2010 to 63% in 2018), Ireland remains a top performer viewed against the DAC average of 55% in 2018,especially given that all its funds are disbursed as grants; the DAC average for the use of country systems for grants is 36% (OECD/UNDP, 2019[3]).

Ireland also limits the number of the conditions it places on its partners. Financing agreements focus, as far as possible, on ensuring that results are drawn from partner countries' own commitments as reflected in their strategies and plans.

Ireland is considered an open and transparent donor, and has some scope to further strengthen its medium-term predictability for the benefit of its partner countries

Partner country governments perceive Ireland as an open and transparent donor. It provides information to country-led aid information platforms in 70% of countries that reported on Ireland in the 2018 GPEDC monitoring round (OECD/UNDP, 2019[3]). As seen in Ethiopia, Ireland also actively supports the management and improvement of such platforms, for example by reflecting more information on effectiveness indicators, and also works to keep such platforms manageable and well aligned to partner country governments' needs. Ireland also places emphasis on capacity building for data at country level in areas of priority for Ireland, for example nutrition data. It also does this through diverse means, including through support to civil society and community-based organisations.

While Ireland is committed to budget predictability through the use of multi-annual funding frameworks, it does not regularly make available forward-looking expenditure plans. Disbursements, however, occur on an annual basis. In its contributions to the public sector, Ireland continues to perform well in terms of annual predictability, with most funds (95%) disbursed within the same year for which they were originally budgeted (against the DAC average of 85%). Regarding medium-term predictability, however, Ireland remains among the bottom group of DAC members; it makes 26% of forward-looking expenditure plans available to partner countries (against the DAC average of 65%), a sharp decline from the 52% share in 2016 (OECD/UNDP, 2019[3]). Ireland establishes indicative estimates of the ODA envelopes it reserves for bilateral programming in mission strategies for their whole period (usually five years) and disaggregated by year. Systematically sharing these with partner countries – with the caveat of annual budget approval – would improve the predictability of Ireland's aid.

Table 5.1. Ireland's results in the 2018 Global Partnership monitoring round

	Alignment and ownership by partner country (%)				Predictability (%)		Transparency		
	SDG 17.15 Use of country-led results frameworks	Funding recorded in countries' national budgets	Funding through countries' systems	Untied ODA	Annual predictability	Medium-term predictability	Retrospective statistics (OECD CRS)	Information for forecasting (OECD FSS)	Publishing to IATI
2016 round	68.80%	90.70%	62%	100%	88.70%	51.70%	Needs improvement	Excellent	Needs improvement
2018 round	54.50%	78.10%	62.90%	100%	94.60%	25.80%	Good	Good	Needs improvement
Trend	-	-	+	=	+	-	+	-	=

Note: CRS = Creditor Reporting System; FSS = Forward Spending Plans; IATI = International Aid Transparency Initiative.
Source: (OECD/UNDP, 2019[3]), *Making Development Co-operation More Effective: 2019 Progress Report*, https://doi.org/10.1787/26f2638f-en.

References

AdaptationWatch (Weikmans et al.) (2016), *Toward transparency: The 2016 Adaptation Finance Transparency Gap Report*, http://www.adaptationwatch.org.   [5]

Dag Hammarskjöld Foundation/UN (2019), *Financing the UN Development System: Time for Hard Choices*, Dag Hammarskjöld Foundation, Uppsala, Sweden/United Nations, New York, https://www.daghammarskjold.se/wp-content/uploads/2019/09/financial-instr-report-2019-interactive.pdf.   [1]

Department of Foreign Affairs and Trade, Ireland (2017), *Irish Aid 2017 Annual Report*, https://www.irishaid.ie/media/irishaid/publications/Irish-Aid-Annual-Report-2017.pdf.   [2]

OECD/UNDP (2019), *Making Development Co-operation More Effective: 2019 Progress Report*, OECD Publishing, Paris, https://doi.org/10.1787/26f2638f-en.   [3]

Publish What You Fund (2019), *The Aid Transparency Index 2018*, https://www.publishwhatyoufund.org/the-index/2018/.   [4]

Notes

[1] When developing in-country strategies, Ireland consulted the private sector in only two out of seven (29%) partner countries reporting in the 2018 Global Partnership for Effective Development Co-operation monitoring round. See (OECD/UNDP, 2019[3]) at https://doi.org/10.1787/26f2638f-en.

[2] The GPEDC monitoring data show a decrease from 91% in 2015 to 64% in 2017 (OECD/UNDP, 2019[3]).

6 Ireland's results, evaluation and learning

This chapter considers the extent to which Ireland assesses the results of its development co-operation; uses the findings of evaluations to feed into decision making, accountability and learning; and assists its partner countries to do the same.

It begins with a look at Ireland's system for managing development results, i.e. whether the objectives of its development co-operation policies and programmes can be measured and assessed from output to impact. The chapter then reviews the alignment of Ireland's evaluation system to the DAC evaluation principles, looking specifically at whether an evaluation policy is in place, whether roles and responsibilities are clear, and whether the process is impartial and independent. Finally, it explores whether there is systematic and transparent dissemination of results, evaluation findings and lessons and whether Ireland learns from both failure and success and communicates what it has achieved and learned.

In brief

Ireland is developing an Accountability Framework to track progress on implementing commitments undertaken in *A Better World*. Focusing mainly on the accountability function, the Framework will not capture corporate results information. However, Ireland plans to develop a more comprehensive result-based management approach in the future. Its commitment to results-based management remains strong, with the monitoring system having significantly improved since the last peer review and results information being used to adapt programmes' design and implementation. Performance measurement frameworks at embassy level are also a helpful tool to track results, although missions vary in their approach and capacity for monitoring and evaluation.

The Evaluation and Audit Unit (EAU), responsible for the evaluation function, is independent and reports directly to the Secretary General of the Department of Foreign Affairs and Trade. A dedicated Evaluation Policy is forthcoming. Centralised evaluations focus mainly on corporate and thematic issues, covering a strategic selection of topics and responding to specific needs. A recent staffing increase allows the EAU to expand its engagement and start supporting business units and partners, particularly to strengthen their evaluative capacity. However, high staff turnover in the EAU remains a concern for evaluation planning.

Ireland is committed to learning. It uses results information for learning and to inform corrective actions. It also disseminates evaluation findings systematically. The EAU tracks implementation of the recommendations made in its evaluations. However, learning is often limited to the team that generated it. There is also a risk that knowledge is lost, especially due to the high staff turnover. If Ireland moves ahead with plans to increase its ODA programme, knowledge management will need to improve.

Management for development results

Ireland is developing a top-level Accountability Framework for A Better World but will not adopt a more comprehensive results-based management approach until afterwards

Ireland is developing an Accountability Framework that will reflect whole-of-government efforts to track progress on implementing *A Better World*. The new framework is intended to identify responsibilities and time frames for the implementation of commitments set out in the new international development policy (Chapter 2). Moreover, the framework will support accountability and reporting across the government – within the Department of Foreign Affairs and Trade (DFAT), between government departments, and to the Cabinet – and it will help the expanded Inter-departmental Committee (IDC) on development co-operation in its monitoring functions (Chapter 4).

The Accountability Framework will focus exclusively on monitoring. It will track progress on the implementation of 20-35 key commitments contained in *A Better World* including the launch of 15 new initiatives as well as new development strategies, resource commitments and changes in the way of doing things.[1] Also the proposed indicators are input-driven rather than outcome and impact level indicators (e.g. the amount of funding provided to education or approval of a strategy). As a result, the Accountability Framework will not have management nor learning functions.

Ireland plans to develop a comprehensive, result-based management approach in the future. This will ideally establish a link with the 2030 Agenda at target and indicator level (whereas *A Better World* provides a link only at goal level) and spell out the chain of expected results from output to impact. Building the results chain will be a necessary step to fill in the missing middle in the Irish results system and ensure that results tracked at programme, country, thematic and sector levels inform strategic decision making and learning, increase transparency, and facilitate communications at different levels.

At embassy level, performance measurement frameworks are a key tool to track results. In the past, country strategies included extensive results frameworks that were published alongside the country paper; recent mission strategies are more succinct and do not always include a published results framework. The recent performance measurement framework for Tanzania (Embassy of Ireland in Tanzania, 2019[1]) provides a good basis for monitoring and accountability at outcome as well as output level, and it assesses the effectiveness of management systems to support delivery of planned results. This may be a model to replicate in future mission strategies.

Ireland regularly monitors results at programme level and uses these to adapt programme design and implementation

Ireland has a strong commitment to results-based management and has shown progress in this regard since the last peer review. It has further institutionalised results approaches in several business processes, including business planning, budgeting and grant management. Under *One World, One Future*, the Framework for Action allowed clarity on key results areas, influencing programming and policy guidance. In 2015, the Development Cooperation and Africa Division (DCAD) organised a dedicated workshop to update its approach to results-based management. The annual budget submitted to the IDC is more focused on results; it identifies outputs and outcomes, the Sustainable Development Goals addressed, and the targeted top policy priorities for every budget line. The government's 2018 annual report on its official development assistance (Government of Ireland, 2019[2]) presents examples of results from country programmes, humanitarian assistance, civil society funding and Ireland's multilateral engagement, including core funding.

The monitoring system has significantly improved, thanks in part to the introduction of a Standard Approach to Grant Management (SAGM). In particular, the SAGM has improved the documentation of grant-level performance, allowing formalised and evidence-based decisions. Grant managers are tasked to record results that will inform performance assessment and/or lessons learned. This allows needed data to be generated in a timely manner, easing the burden on implementing partners (Department of Foreign Affairs and Trade, Ireland, 2017[3]).[2] In addition, partnership arrangements, such as the Programme Grant II with Irish civil society organisations, give significant importance to applicants' approach to results and learning (Department of Foreign Affairs and Trade, Ireland, 2017[4]). Ireland also regularly communicates with multilaterals to collect results information of its core contributions.

Staff use results information at programme level to adapt design and implementation, but there is room to increase adaptability. Although missions vary in their approach and specialised capacity for monitoring,[3] programmes undergo regular reviews (every six months, annually and at mid-term), with the mid-term reviews used to inform possible programme management changes. Ireland thus ensures a certain degree of flexibility in programme implementation. Nevertheless, it plans to move further in the direction of adaptive management by enhancing the flexibility already built into programmes and shifting the focus of grant approval away from "what DCAD will do" and to "how decisions will be managed" (Government of Ireland, 2019[5]).

Ireland occasionally supports partner countries in building their statistical capacity but is decreasing its use of partner countries' data

Ireland channels funding through United Nations (UN) agencies to strengthen the capacities of national statistic bodies. In Tanzania, for example, it supports UN Women and the UN Children's Fund to strengthen capacity of the national statistic bodies, including the National Bureau of Statistics, on generation and use of data from social institutions to inform evidence-based policies on gender equality and women's empowerment and on nutrition.

However, Ireland is decreasing its use of partner country governments' data and statistics to monitor its own strategies and programmes. Ireland's use of results indicators that are monitored using government sources and monitoring systems decreased from 50% in 2016 to 45% in 2018 (OECD/UNDP, 2019[6]).

Evaluation system

Ireland uses its independent evaluation function strategically

The Evaluation and Audit Unit is independent and reports directly to the Secretary General of DFAT. Its work plan and products are reviewed by an independent Audit Committee, which advises the Secretary General and whose reports are provided to the Comptroller and Auditor General. The EAU is a member of the Irish Government Economic and Evaluation Services network (IGEES) and as such, benefits from additional support from the economists of the network. Ireland considers the combination of evaluation and audit functions in the same unit as a strength. Through this, DFAT brings development affinity to the audit function, which otherwise might become too risk-averse. Nevertheless, there is a separation of roles between evaluation and auditing staff.

The EAU conducts and commissions centralised evaluations and promotes findings. A three-year Evaluation Strategic Plan guides the functioning of the EAU (Department of Foreign Affairs and Trade, Ireland, 2017[7]) and a dedicated Evaluation Policy is under development. As a unit serving the whole of DFAT, the EAU also supports other business units in the department. However, two thirds of its evaluations focus on development co-operation.

Selection of centralised evaluations ensures that they cover a strategic selection of topics and respond to specific information needs. The EAU selects evaluations among proposals received by all business units on the basis of a clear set of criteria, including among others utility, relevance, innovativeness, feasibility and timeliness. Evaluations are selected prioritising those areas of DFAT's expenditure where evaluation coverage is weaker and then narrowing down the specific focus through consultations. To ensure responding to longer term needs, a three-year evaluation plan is then endorsed by the Senior Management Group and approved by the DFAT Secretary General. Evaluations have a dedicated budget line, although the business units involved may contribute to costs.

The EAU's evaluative focus is on corporate and thematic evaluations. Every mission strategy is evaluated about one and a half years before expiration to inform internal financial controls and reflections on the new strategy (Chapter 2). This exercise has a dual purpose of accountability and learning. The EAU also carries out or co-ordinates evaluations on themes and a few selected programmes, although few of these were conducted in recent years due to limited capacity and more are due according to the current three-year plan.

Other business units and missions can undertake or commission decentralised evaluations based on their learning and accountability needs. According to the SAGM, grant evaluations are optional depending on the quality and content of progress reports. Ireland does not publish decentralised evaluations. The unit director or grant manager is responsible for disseminating the findings among relevant stakeholders.

A recent staff increase could enable the EAU to support missions and partners regarding the quality and use of evaluations and to scale up its engagement

Insufficient human resources impacted Ireland's evaluation activities in the aftermath of the financial crisis. In 2014, the DFAT evaluation function had a staff equivalent to four and a half, dropping in 2015 to a minimum of one. The EAU again reached sufficient capacity in September 2019, with a staff of seven people dedicated to evaluation. Before this, the EAU was limited in its capacity to provide advisory services to missions and partners or to carry out joint evaluations. The EAU had also begun to only contract evaluations to external consultants, but started in 2017 to undertake evaluations using mixed teams of external consultants and EAU staff to ensure consistent levels of quality.

The staff increase allows the EAU to expand its engagement and start supporting business units, particularly to strengthen their evaluative capacity. Ireland actively participates in international networks, such as the DAC Evaluation Network, European Union networks and Nordic+, and is a member of the Multilateral Organisation Performance Assessment Network. Recently, it started to work with Finland and Switzerland to undertake a mutual review of their respective evaluation functions, the strategic fit of these functions in the member ministry, and their good practices and areas for improvement. This will help to improve Ireland's evaluation system. The EAU has also started to rebuild and restructure itself. This process includes revising its internal quality assurance systems, developing new research methodologies, ensuring adequate training provision and developing new policy and guidelines.

However, staff turnover in the EAU remains a risk that affects evaluation planning. The competencies required of good evaluators are developed over time. As Ireland transfers staff from other roles in DFAT into the EAU, an assignment to the EAU comes with a steep learning curve and should thus be of sufficient duration both to allow officers time to acquire these skills and to enable DFAT to capture a return of its training investment.

Institutional learning

Ireland is committed to learning, but knowledge is not shared across teams, units and missions in a systematic way

Ireland is committed to learning and a culture of self-reflection is widespread. The formulation of every new mission strategy builds on extensive reflections, external analysis and an evaluation of the previous strategy (Chapter 2). The EAU is frequently involved in conducting reviews before management decisions are taken. Internal and external consultations also often inform decision making. Grants are regularly scrutinised and monitored and, as discussed, Ireland uses results information for learning purposes as well as to inform corrective actions.

The EAU systematically disseminates centralised evaluation findings and tracks implementation of recommendations. Findings are presented to key internal stakeholders, the partner being evaluated, the DCAD Senior Management Group (and/or Management Board), the Audit Committee, and the partner government in the case of mission strategy evaluations. DFAT also publishes reports of centralised evaluations on its website. All evaluations and reviews require a management response and the EAU now tracks the follow-up to these responses. Tracking was re-introduced in 2019 after it was suspended due to low staffing levels beforehand.

However, learning is often limited to the strategy or programme in question, as knowledge remains by and large within the team that created it. For example, even though grant managers identify and document lessons through the SAGM, learning is not captured by a broader knowledge management system in a way that could inform decisions in other parts of DFAT. Exchanges of information across teams often rely on informal staff collaboration and co-ordination.

High staff turnover and plans to grow the development programme raise the risk that knowledge is lost, making better knowledge management all the more important. Ireland is committed to improve institutional knowledge management and could start with scaling up existing good practices that build on the strong networking culture. These include structured mechanisms to facilitate exchanges among staff, such as regional thematic workshops, and formal communities of practice. Ireland could also make information on specific knowledge and experience available so that staff can identify whom to contact (i.e. transactive memory). Improved information technology infrastructure and e-based processes could dramatically facilitate knowledge exchange between missions and headquarters and better enable institutional learning. Ireland also recognises the need to scale up policy-relevant research – the review of the *Research Strategy 2015-2019* will inform an expanded, multi-stream approach with clear operational guidance for research, evidence, knowledge and learning (Chapter 2).

Ireland could draw lessons on knowledge management from the experience of other DAC members. The Japan International Cooperation Agency, for example, has built up a comprehensive and public database on lessons learned from evaluations to inform project design. It also runs 22 communities of practice for knowledge exchange across the agency. The thematic sections of the Australian Department of Foreign Affairs and Trade synthesise lessons from Australia's co-operation and research and adapt them for diverse users. They use digital collaboration platforms to link thematic expertise with knowledge generated in the field, facilitating networking, disseminating performance stories as well as key messages for media opportunities.

References

Department of Foreign Affairs and Trade, Ireland (2017), *Appraisers' Guide for the Programme Grant II (2017-2022) and the Humanitarian Programme Plan (2017-2018) (internal document)*. [4]

Department of Foreign Affairs and Trade, Ireland (2017), *Evaluation Strategic Plan 2017-2019 (internal document)*. [7]

Department of Foreign Affairs and Trade, Ireland (2017), *Standard Approach to Grant Management in DCAD*. [3]

Embassy of Ireland in Tanzania (2019), *Mission Strategy Performance Measurement Framework*, Government of Ireland, Dublin. [1]

Government of Ireland (2019), *DAC Peer Review 2020: Memorandum of Ireland*. [5]

Government of Ireland (2019), *Official Development Assistance: Annual Report 2018*, https://www.irishaid.ie/media/irishaid/latestnews/Irish-Aid-2018-Annual-Report.pdf. [2]

OECD/UNDP (2019), *Making Development Co-operation More Effective: 2019 Progress Report*, OECD Publishing, Paris, https://doi.org/10.1787/26f2638f-en. [6]

Notes

[1] One of the new initiatives is "creating a funding initiative for women's economic empowerment with a focus on agriculture"; an example of a resource commitment in the policy document is to "scale up funding to education especially for girls in emergencies, committing to spending at least EUR 250 million over the next five years".

[2] According to the SAGM, implementing partners are not required to report against the corporate results framework but should provide regular progress updates on the basis of an agreed set of results.

[3] The peer review team noted that additional monitoring and evaluation expertise at the embassy level, together with support from headquarters, would be helpful.

7 Ireland's approach to fragility, crises and humanitarian assistance

This chapter first reviews Ireland's efforts to engage in fragile, conflict and crisis contexts. It assesses Ireland's political directives and strategies for working in these contexts; the extent to which programmes are designed coherently to address key drivers of fragility, conflict and disaster risk; and the needs of women and the most vulnerable; and whether systems, processes and people work together effectively in responding to crises.

The second part of the chapter considers Ireland's efforts to fulfil the principles and good practices of humanitarian donorship. It looks at the political directives and strategies for humanitarian assistance; the effectiveness of Ireland's humanitarian programming and whether it targets the highest risk to life and livelihoods; and whether approaches and partnerships ensure high-quality assistance.

In brief

Ireland is a key actor on the global policy stage, backing up its global commitments with special efforts on important issues such as United Nations (UN) reform and the Women, Peace and Security Agenda. *A Better World* has a strong focus on fragility and reducing humanitarian need in line with the push by Ireland to reach the furthest behind first. Allocations follow intentions: In 2017, 57.5% of the country's official development assistance was allocated to fragile contexts.

Ireland has a unique approach to crises and fragility that builds on learning, including from its troubled past, and focuses on key issues such as refugees and migration and gender. A good range of tools – diplomatic, development and humanitarian – ensure that Ireland can design an appropriate response to individual fragile contexts. Efforts to clarify Ireland's risk appetite in fragile contexts and to scale up conflict prevention programming would be useful.

Ireland is widely seen as an excellent partner, providing quality financing and supporting its investments with a presence on key partner bodies such as boards and donor support groups where Ireland uses its influence to improve effectiveness and coherence. There are good efforts to align internal funding streams to support the humanitarian-development-peace nexus. Ireland could now continue to improve its coherence with other humanitarian, development and peace actors on the ground.

A Better World provides a clear mandate for Irish humanitarian assistance, and is working to translate this into strategic and operational guidance for the humanitarian programme.

Ireland allocates its funding to partners and then focuses on supporting those partners to increase their effectiveness and programmes, with a focus on the furthest behind. Progress has been made on monitoring and communications following the 2014 peer review recommendation. Ireland's intentions to further strengthen links between partner performance and future funding allocations should be encouraged.

Ireland has a good range of rapid response and protracted crisis tools, and is a very progressive donor in terms of predictable and flexible financing. It would be useful to document Ireland's experience and good practice in this area – including what this quality funding has allowed partners to improve – to make the case for this kind of financing to other DAC members.

The model for Ireland's humanitarian programme is built on its influencing power, and for this, Ireland must have staff with the right knowledge and skills in key positions. However, almost without exception, partners report that Ireland seems stretched in its global engagements. Ireland will need to take care that it invests in the needed staffing capacities to retain credibility and influencing power.

7.A Crises and fragility

Strategic framework

Ireland uses its good offices to advance global efforts on crises and fragility

Ireland takes its role as a global standard-bearer for better policy on crises and fragility very seriously. The Irish approach involves leading global efforts on key policy issues, as well as encouraging the multilateral system to do better in terms of delivery. In both aspects, Ireland certainly has more influence than its financial weight would suggest. Notable actions include Ireland's promotion of the Women, Peace and Security agenda both internationally and domestically (Chapter 1) (Government of Ireland, 2019[1]); its launch of the OECD flagship publication, *States of Fragility,* in 2018; its proactive diplomacy to support the good offices role of UN Resident Coordinators during the UN reform process; its active membership of the Peacebuilding Commission; and its leadership role on donor support groups and boards, including as the:

- 2018 chair of the United Nations Office for the Coordination of Humanitarian Affairs donor support group
- 2015-2016 chair of the Pooled Fund Working Group, where Ireland facilitated the development of the common performance framework
- 2019 chair of the International Committee of the Red Cross (ICRC) donor support group.

Ireland's development co-operation policy focuses *strongly on fragility and reducing humanitarian need*

***A Better World* focuses on the furthest behind first and the importance of reducing humanitarian need by addressing its key drivers, conflict and fragility** (Government of Ireland, 2019[2]). The policy calls for greater investment in conflict prevention, tackling root causes, peacekeeping, and the gender aspects of peace and security. *A Better World* thus constitutes a useful framework for Ireland's overall programming and advocacy efforts across the government.

Ireland's allocations largely follow its policy commitments to address crises and fragility

In 2018, 55.5% of Irish official development assistance (ODA) was allocated to fragile contexts,[1] well above the average of 38% for all DAC donors. However, the share has been declining each year since 2013, when allocations to fragile contexts made up from 67.9% of Ireland's total ODA. Ireland will need to take care to ensure that its allocations match its policy ambitions. In terms of the humanitarian-development-peace nexus, 28% of Ireland's ODA to fragile contexts goes to humanitarian assistance and 11% to peace, which is roughly consistent with the average share to these areas allocated by other DAC members (OECD, n.d.[3]).

Effective programme design and instruments

Ireland's history provides the backdrop for its unique approach to crises and fragility

Although there is no formal cross-government mechanism guiding Ireland's engagement in fragile contexts, there is general coherence across Irish efforts. This is largely driven by Ireland's history. For instance, Ireland drew on its experience with the Good Friday Agreement to push for the participation of women in peace processes. However, a more deliberate co-ordination around Ireland's approach to fragility would be beneficial, for example by ensuring the close alignment of Department of Defence contributions to peacekeeping; Department of Finance work on World Bank International Development Association replenishments; Department of Agriculture, Food and the Marine support to the Rome-based agencies; and the development co-operation programme of the Department of Foreign Affairs and Trade (DFAT). Efforts to build a more systematic common Irish approach, as reflected in *A Better World*, are to be encouraged and are especially important as the development co-operation programme grows.

There is potential for more conflict prevention programming

Ireland's tools for programme design are well adapted to developing a risk-informed strategy for individual fragile contexts. In particular, the poverty and vulnerability approach to programming allows Ireland to identify drivers of fragility and ensure that power dynamics are considered, i.e. working politically to complement development inputs. Regularly sharing learning and experience (both good and bad) from Ireland's peace process with key actors in fragile and crisis contexts – the peer review team heard many examples of this occurring – is one clear demonstration of Ireland's approach to thinking and working politically. As is the case for other donors, more could be done to develop a systematic approach to conflict prevention, across both development co-operation and diplomatic tools. Ireland has a useful toolbox for fragility and crises.

Ireland's fragility toolbox includes a useful mix of ODA and non-ODA diplomatic, development, peace and humanitarian tools. On the diplomatic side, sharing experiences from the Northern Ireland peace process – often under the radar for political sensitivity reasons – has proven useful in a variety of conflict situations. Development tools allow for un-earmarked funding to key partners and funds, including the Peacebuilding Fund, alongside targeted capacity-building interventions. On peace, Ireland is the largest per-capita contributor to peacekeeping missions, and a Stability Fund finances peace programming to a range of partners, now on a multi-annual basis. Humanitarian financing is to a large extent provided on a multi-annual basis, with some financing tools now potentially moving to five-year multi-annual cycles to align with development programming and thus facilitate the nexus; this is a progressive approach that other donors could learn from. Risk appetite is one area where Ireland could firm up its approach and it is critical, given planned budget increases (Chapter 4). Working in fragile contexts is inherently risky, results are less sure, and the cost of delivering in risky environments may run counter to traditional views of value for money. DFAT has not yet elaborated its risk appetite nor communicated on this to the Irish public. Doing so would provide useful clarity to partners and is thus to be encouraged.

Ireland took a lead role in the New York Declaration

Ireland played a key role in shepherding the New York Declaration for Refugees and Migrants and related compacts, which represented a useful contribution to global public goods. Ireland also contributes to European Union (EU) trust funds in this area to demonstrate solidarity with its EU partners. But migration, and particularly the EU's approach to migration, is an area where Ireland's values and interests do not always correspond with their EU partners. Ireland's efforts to promote a principled approach to refugees and migrants in multilateral settings – including the DAC – are thus much appreciated.

Gender issues are a key focus

A Better World **makes a significant commitment to gender equality, and this plays out in Ireland's fragility and crisis programming.** Ireland leads on the gender aspects of peacekeeping reform. It also has a strong global voice, policy and programming focus on Women, Peace and Security and is working on this through its humanitarian programming; for example, it is using its leadership role on ICRC donor support group to focus on sexual and gender based violence. Ireland's role on gender equality issues in these contexts is much appreciated by partners.

Effective delivery and partnerships

Predictable, flexible financing underpins a strategic approach to partnership

Ireland's approach to partnership in the fragility and crisis space is to provide long-term, flexible funds – up to three years for humanitarian partners and five years for peacebuilding – to allow partners the freedom and predictability to tailor responses to evolving crisis contexts. This is good practice. Interestingly, Ireland then adds value to these partner funds through its own diplomatic efforts. These efforts take the form of sharing its experiences from its own peace processes, as noted, and using its presence and influence on organisation boards and donor support groups to nudge partners to do better. On the ground, Ireland backs its investments with engagement, for example through the new embassy in Jordan to cover the regional aspects of the Syria crisis. It also seeks coherence on the global stage, for example by seeking to connect the Peacebuilding Fund and the work of the Peacebuilding Commission, which Ireland joined in 2019. This overall approach is highly strategic, allowing Ireland, as a moderate-size donor, to gain maximum benefit from its fragility investments.

Efforts to deliver the DAC recommendation on the nexus are promising

Alongside the other DAC members, Ireland adhered to the DAC *Recommendation on Humanitarian-Development-Peace Nexus* in February 2019. In line with this recommendation, Ireland is already making good efforts to promote coherence across funding streams involved in fragile contexts, including through:

- concurrent application and appraisal processes for non-governmental organisation (NGO) funding across development and humanitarian funding streams
- including the humanitarian programme and budget in country strategies
- raising the nexus in discussions with major partners
- accepting joint humanitarian and development reports from partners
- reflections on extending multi-annual funding to humanitarian partners to five years, to match the development cycle.

There are opportunities for Ireland to go further as it looks to deliver on commitments under the DAC recommendation. These opportunities include greater links with the Defence Forces where they are present, for example as part of peacekeeping missions. But such opportunities centre around enhancing Ireland's coherence with other actors on the ground – bilateral, multilateral and civil society – in recognition that the nexus is about coherence of the international community's efforts as a whole, not just Ireland's efforts. Ireland is encouraged to continue its efforts in this regard and to share its learning with the wider DAC community.

7.B Humanitarian assistance

Humanitarian assistance strategic framework

Humanitarian efforts are recognised in A Better World

Humanitarian programming is given priority in *A Better World* as part of Ireland's ambition to reduce humanitarian need. Given the principles behind the DAC *Recommendation on Humanitarian-Development-Peace Nexus*, it is good practice for humanitarian and development programming in fragile and crisis-affected contexts to be guided by one overarching policy statement.

Ireland is now working to develop strategic and operational guidance to translate *A Better World* into its humanitarian programme. In conjunction with this, it will be interesting to watch efforts to determine what the global aspiration of reaching the furthest behind first means for the humanitarian programme and its related implications for the cost of response and the risks that need to be taken to respond to this often hard-to-reach group (Chapter 2).

Effective humanitarian programming

In line with its overall approach, Ireland allocates funds by partner (the who) rather than by where and what, and then seeks to improve effectiveness

Ireland sees itself as a true partner to the humanitarian community and accordingly a significant proportion of its funding allocations are by partner. Overall, approximately 30% of its allocations go to the Central Emergency Response Fund and country-based pooled funds, 30% to UN agencies, 20% to the EU, 12% to NGOs, and 8% to the ICRC, with the majority of this funding (53% in 2019) not earmarked to particular crises or sectors (Government of Ireland, 2019[4]). This is in line with the importance Ireland places on a rules-based global system. Ireland then works to ensure that partner programming is effective and needs-based, for example through its work to improve the quality of Humanitarian Response Plans and to develop the common performance framework for pooled funds. A smaller proportion of the envelope, approximately 30%, allows Ireland to target geographically, based on the severity of need, using tools such as the INFORM risk index, and selecting partners – mainly country based pooled funds, UN and NGOs – based on their track records in those contexts. This is good practice. Ireland does not make direct allocations to local partners, preferring instead to encourage its partners, especially NGOs and pooled funds, to pass funds through to local actors.

Monitoring and reporting have improved

The 2014 peer review recommended that Ireland move towards more systematic publication of its own reviews and results, and there has been progress in this direction, including a new section in the annual report. The new grant management system may help bring about further transparency in the future. A thematic evaluation of the humanitarian programme in relation to the humanitarian business plan is under consideration. This is to be encouraged. Partner reporting has been simplified. For the most part, Ireland accepts partner standard reports, supplementing them with field visits for real-time monitoring. Work has already begun to link partner performance to future allocations and this, too, is to be encouraged. It might also be useful to review the reporting and administrative burden due to reporting requirements from NGO partners, against those Ireland requires of the UN system. A move instead to a more risk-based approach might be considered.

Effective delivery, partnerships and instruments of humanitarian assistance

Ireland has a solid rapid response toolbox

As noted in the previous peer review, Ireland has a range of tools for rapid response. The most useful is prepositioned funding with a core group of Irish NGOs, under its Emergency Response Funding Scheme. Funding to NGOs is sometimes supplemented by calls for proposals, with a rapid turnaround, for specific issues, as was recently done for Ebola in Democratic Republic of the Congo. Ireland also supports the in-kind stocks of the Humanitarian Response Depots, although staff informed the peer review team that this would be reviewed in light of the global push towards greater cash programming and for local purchases of response items.

Ireland is doing better than most DAC members on multi-annual funding

Ireland's funding arrangements are considered of high quality. In 2017, 42% of Ireland's humanitarian funding was multi-year funding – up to three years for NGOs under the Humanitarian Programme Plan – and 53% was un-earmarked or only softly earmarked. This quality funding allows partners to plan ahead, include resilience approaches, save money and retain key staff. Ireland could usefully collect some of these success stories and share them with other, more reluctant, donors. Even funding through other government departments is highly predictable and flexible, as is the case in relationship of the Department of Agriculture, Food and the Marine with the World Food Programme. Partners across the board are highly appreciative of Ireland's engagement and the quality of funding arrangements.

Organisation fit for purpose

Ireland must make sure it has the right staff in place and that they are not overstretched

Ireland's humanitarian programme model is laudably based on the ability to have strategic influence at the highest levels of the global humanitarian system. This approach is to be commended and is effective. However, the approach is dependent on Ireland having sufficient staff with deep humanitarian knowledge and influencing skills in key positions. Almost without exception, partners interviewed for this review noted that despite excellent quality staff across the board, Ireland is often stretched with its leadership role on many boards and donor support groups and in global processes such as the Grand Bargain falling on a small number of key staff spread across Ireland, Ankara, Nairobi, New York and Geneva. In addition, staff are cycled in and out of posts regularly, increasing the strain on those remaining while new staff get up to speed. This overstretching – whether real or perceived – risks harming Ireland's credibility in the policy space, which will in turn impact its influencing potential. Ireland will need to reflect on ensuring that humanitarian staff have the right expertise to develop the appropriate trust and gravitas that will ensure it retains influencing power and thus delivers to the full potential of the Irish humanitarian model.

Communication

Improvements in communications

Ireland has committed to improving its external communications, including through the Government of Ireland's annual report on development co-operation, parliamentary questions and social media. The government engages with the media when there are high-level visits, particularly from the UN, to Ireland. Going forward, Ireland could look at updating its website with a view to also sharing information about its own progress – for example on Grand Bargain commitments – rather than in more publicity-focused media work.

References

Government of Ireland (2019), *A Better World: Ireland's Policy for International Development*, [2]
https://www.irishaid.ie/media/irishaid/aboutus/abetterworldirelandspolicyforinternationaldevelopment/A-Better-World-Irelands-Policy-for-International-Development.pdf.

Government of Ireland (2019), *DAC Peer Review 2020: Memorandum of Ireland*. [4]

Government of Ireland (2019), *Women, Peace and Security: Ireland's Third National Action Plan for the Implementation of UNSCR 1325 and Related Resolutions, 2019-2024*, https://www.dfa.ie/media/dfa/ourrolepolicies/womenpeaceandsecurity/Third-National-Action-Plan.pdf.   [1]

OECD (n.d.), *States of Fragility Platform*, http://www3.compareyourcountry.org/states-of-fragility/overview/0/.   [3]

Notes

[1] Gross disbursements basis.

Annex A. Progress since the 2014 DAC peer review recommendations

Towards a comprehensive Irish development effort

Recommendations 2014	Progress
To deliver on its commitment to policy coherence for development, Ireland can build on its whole of government approaches to develop a clear cross-government plan of action on a few policy issues of strategic priority which it can influence.	Partially implemented

Vision and policies for development co-operation

Recommendations 2014	Progress
DFAT's guidance and tools for taking decisions about programming and partnerships should provide clarity of purpose, help rationalise delivery of the programme and take staffing capacity into account.	Implemented
The Irish Government should set out its ambition and priorities for all its multilateral engagement and use these to guide strategic allocations to multilateral organisations.	Partially implemented
DFAT should clarify how it will operationalise the One World, One Future priority on inclusive economic growth and define the coherence and linkages with the Africa Strategy's trade objective. It can learn from DAC members' experience in this area.	Partially implemented

Aid volume and allocation

Recommendations 2014	Progress
Ireland should communicate the rationale and projections for scaling up its ODA towards 0.7% of GNI to the public and key stakeholders. It should also start planning how increases will be allocated.	Partially implemented

Organisation and management

Recommendations 2014	Progress
DFAT should finalise its human resource policy for development co-operation staff and introduce medium-term workforce planning to ensure it has the right levels of staff and competencies to deliver its policy and respond to field imperatives.	Partially implemented
DCD should ensure that more standardised management	Implemented

systems produce information that is relevant for, and feeds into, context-specific strategic planning.	

Development co-operation delivery and partnerships

Recommendations 2014	Progress
Ireland should continue to deliver locally owned development co-operation aligned to partners' priorities and work with development providers to push for effective delivery of international commitments for making aid effective.	Partially implemented
To deliver on the trade and economic growth objectives of *One World, One Future* and the Africa Strategy, Ireland needs rigorous analysis, a clear policy and the right tools and instruments for effective engagement with the private sector.	Partially implemented
Embassies and NGOs receiving support from headquarters should work together to improve dialogue and co-ordination for more effective programming in the partner country.	Implemented

Results and accountability

Recommendations 2014	Progress
DFAT should build on the work underway to strengthen its information management systems, creating a culture of learning and investing in knowledge sharing.	Partially implemented
Ireland should further improve the transparency of its development co-operation.	Implemented

Humanitarian assistance

Recommendations 2014	Progress
To improve predictability, Ireland should ensure that its eligibility criteria and procedures for the various humanitarian funding schemes are better communicated.	Partially implemented
Ireland should work towards more systematic publication of both its programme reviews and the results of its humanitarian programme.	Partially implemented

Figure A.1. Ireland's implementation of 2014 peer review recommendations

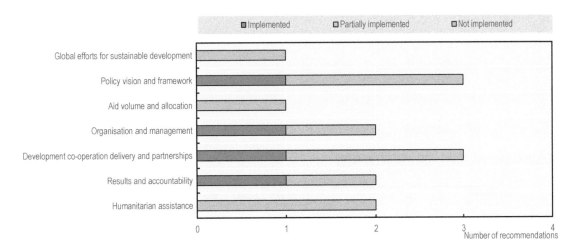

Annex B. OECD/DAC standard suite of tables

Table B.1. Total financial flows

USD million at current prices and exchange rates

Ireland	2004-08	2009-13	2014	2015	2016	2017	2018
							Grant equivalent
ODA grant equivalent	..	..	..	-	-	-	934
ODA grant equivalent (at constant 2017 USD million)	..	..	..	-	-	-	891
ODA grant equivalent (as a % of GNI)	..	..	..	..	..	..	0.31
							Net disbursements
Total official flows	974	894	816	718	803	838	934
Official development assistance	974	894	816	718	803	838	934
Bilateral	656	593	519	427	427	493	530
Grants	656	593	519	427	427	493	530
Non-grants	-	-	-	- 0	-	-	-
Multilateral	318	301	297	291	376	345	404
Other official flows	-	-	-	-	-	-	-
Bilateral: *of which*	-	-	-	-	-	-	-
Investment-related transactions	-	-	-	-	-	-	-
Multilateral	-	-	-	-	-	-	-
Officially guaranteed export credits	-	-	-	-	-	-	-
Net Private Grants	294	250	388	509	493	364	433
Private flows at market terms	3 997	1 300	-	-	-	-	-
Bilateral: *of which*	3 997	1 300	-	-	-	-	-
Direct investment	-	-	-	-	-	-	-
Multilateral	-	-	-	-	-	-	-
Total flows	5 265	2 443	1 203	1 228	1 295	1 202	1 368
for reference:							
ODA net flows (as a % of GNI)	0.51	0.50	0.38	0.32	0.32	0.32	0.31
ODA net flows (at constant 2017 USD million)	847	808	742	727	821	838	891
Total flows (as a % of GNI) (a)	2.75	1.37	0.55	0.54	0.51	0.46	0.46
ODA to and channelled through NGOs							
- In USD million	266	302	391	184	182	188	200
ODA to and channelled through multilaterals							
- In USD million	407	419	398	370	493	471	547

a. To countries eligible for ODA.

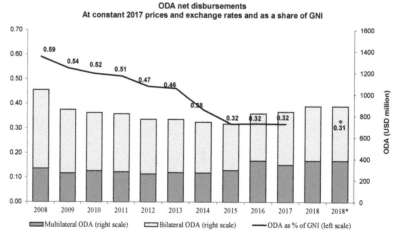

StatLink https://doi.org/10.1787/888934121278

Table B.2. ODA by main categories

Disbursements

Ireland	Constant 2017 USD million					Per cent share of gross disbursements					Total DAC 2017 %
	2014	2015	2016	2017	2018	2014	2015	2016	2017	2018	
Gross Bilateral ODA	**472**	**433**	**437**	**493**	**506**	**64**	**60**	**53**	**59**	**57**	**74**
Budget support	11	16	-	-	-	1	2	-	-	-	2
of which: General budget support	11	16	-	-	-	1	2	-	-	-	1
Core contributions & pooled prog.& funds	250	251	260	287	271	34	35	32	34	30	13
of which: Core support to national NGOs	102	92	90	99	95	14	13	11	12	11	1
Core support to international NGOs	19	19	23	19	21	3	3	3	2	2	0
Core support to PPPs	1	4	5	8	3	0	1	1	1	0	0
Project-type interventions	165	114	126	116	132	22	16	15	14	15	39
of which: Investment projects	-	-	0	1	-	-	-	0	0	-	13
Experts and other technical assistance	10	13	11	9	9	1	2	1	1	1	3
Scholarships and student costs in donor countries	3	3	3	4	3	0	0	0	0	0	2
of which: Imputed student costs	0	-	-	-	0	0	-	-	-	0	1
Debt relief grants	-	-	-	-	-	-	-	-	-	-	0
Administrative costs	30	30	31	31	32	4	4	4	4	4	5
Other in-donor expenditures	3	5	6	45	59	0	1	1	5	7	9
of which: refugees in donor countries	0	1	1	41	54	0	0	0	5	6	9
Gross Multilateral ODA	**270**	**294**	**384**	**345**	**385**	**36**	**40**	**47**	**41**	**43**	**26**
UN agencies	81	90	119	80	102	11	12	14	10	11	4
EU institutions	130	143	206	203	220	18	20	25	24	25	9
World Bank group	23	27	30	31	28	3	4	4	4	3	5
Regional development banks	8	8	7	8	8	1	1	1	1	1	3
Other multilateral	27	27	23	23	27	4	4	3	3	3	6
Total gross ODA	**742**	**727**	**821**	**838**	**891**	**100**	**100**	**100**	**100**	**100**	**100**
of which: Gross ODA loans	6	-	-	-	-	1	-	-	-	-	-
Bilateral	-	-	-	-	-	-	-	-	-	-	-
Multilateral	6	-	-	-	-	1	-	-	-	-	-
Repayments and debt cancellation	-	-	-	-	-						
Total net ODA	**742**	**727**	**821**	**838**	**891**						
For reference:											
Country programmable aid	*220*	*163*	*142*	*152*	*155*						
Free standing technical co-operation	*10*	*17*	*14*	*13*	*25*						
Net debt relief	-	-	-	-	-						

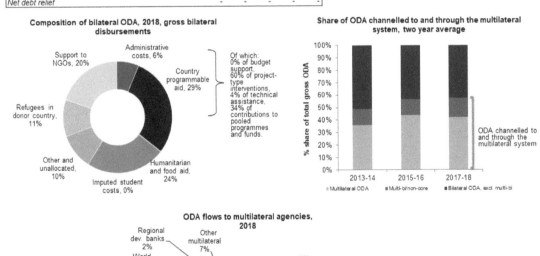

Composition of bilateral ODA, 2018, gross bilateral disbursements

Support to NGOs, 20%; Administrative costs, 6%; Country programmable aid, 29%; Refugees in donor country, 11%; Other and unallocated, 10%; Imputed student costs, 0%; Humanitarian and food aid, 24%

Of which: 0% of budget support, 60% of project-type interventions, 4% of technical assistance, 34% of contributions to pooled programmes and funds.

Share of ODA channelled to and through the multilateral system, two year average

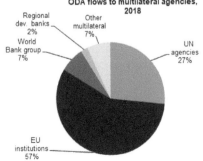

ODA flows to multilateral agencies, 2018

Regional dev. banks 2%; Other multilateral 7%; World Bank group 7%; UN agencies 27%; EU institutions 57%

StatLink https://doi.org/10.1787/888934121297

Table B.3. Bilateral ODA allocable by region and income group

Gross disbursements

Ireland	Constant 2017 USD million					% share					Total DAC 2017%
	2014	2015	2016	2017	2018	2014	2015	2016	2017	2018	
Africa	310	280	257	261	254	81	82	78	78	78	**40**
Sub-Saharan Africa	309	275	256	258	251	81	81	78	77	77	**34**
North Africa	1	1	0	0	0	0	0	0	0	0	**4**
Asia	32	24	22	22	23	8	7	7	7	7	**30**
South and Central Asia	11	9	8	10	10	3	3	3	3	3	**18**
Far East	22	15	14	12	13	6	5	4	4	4	**11**
America	11	10	12	10	9	3	3	4	3	3	**9**
North and Central America	8	8	8	6	6	2	2	3	2	2	**4**
South America	3	2	3	4	4	1	1	1	1	1	**4**
Middle East	27	26	30	25	32	7	8	9	8	10	**13**
Oceania	0	0	-	-	1	0	0	-	-	0	**2**
Europe	1	2	7	15	8	0	1	2	5	2	**5**
Total bilateral allocable by region	382	341	329	334	327	100	100	100	100	100	**100**
Least developed	281	260	244	248	241	76	78	75	75	75	**39**
Other low-income	9	8	8	8	9	2	2	2	2	3	**1**
Lower middle-income	65	52	50	43	48	18	15	16	13	15	**41**
Upper middle-income	13	14	22	30	23	4	4	7	9	7	**19**
More advanced developing countries	-	-	0	0	-	-	-	0	0	-	**0**
Total bilateral allocable by income	369	333	325	329	321	100	100	100	100	100	**100**
For reference[2]:											
Total bilateral	472	433	437	493	506	100	100	100	100	100	**100**
of which: Unallocated by region	90	92	108	159	178	19	21	25	32	35	**32**
of which: Unallocated by income	103	99	112	164	185	22	23	26	33	37	**39**
Fragile and conflict-affected states (as per DCR of each year)	326	301	286	283	281	69	70	66	57	55	**35**
SIDS (as per data provided to UN)	3	3	4	2	2	1	1	1	0	0	**2**
Landlocked developing countries (as per data provided to UN)	165	146	141	144	142	35	34	32	29	28	**14**

1. Each region includes regional amounts which cannot be allocated by sub-region. The sum of the sub-regional amounts may therefore fall short of the regional total.
2. 'Fragile and conflict-affected states' group has overlaps with SIDS and Landlocked developing countries and can therefore not be added. For the same reason, these three groups cannot be added to any income group.

Gross bilateral ODA by income group, 2013-18

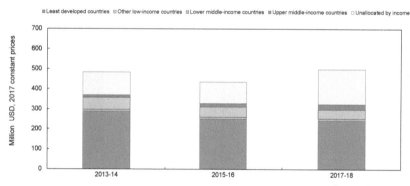

StatLink https://doi.org/10.1787/888934121316

Table B.4. Main recipients of bilateral ODA

2013-14 average

Ireland	Current USD million	Constant 2017 USD mln	% share	Memo: DAC countries' average %
Mozambique	54	49	10	
Ethiopia	47	43	9	
Tanzania	38	35	7	
Uganda	34	31	6	
Malawi	26	24	5	
Top 5 recipients	200	182	38	25
Zambia	25	22	5	
Viet Nam	17	15	3	
Sierra Leone	14	13	3	
South Sudan	11	10	2	
Syrian Arab Republic	10	9	2	
Top 10 recipients	278	253	52	39
Liberia	9	8	2	
Kenya	9	8	2	
Zimbabwe	9	8	2	
Somalia	8	7	1	
West Bank and Gaza Strip	8	7	1	
Top 15 recipients	321	291	60	46
Sudan	7	7	1	
South Africa	6	6	1	
Democratic Republic of the Congo	6	5	1	
Central African Republic	5	4	1	
Congo	5			
Top 20 recipients	350	318	66	52
Total (143 recipients)	408	371	77	
Unallocated	124	113	23	36
Total bilateral gross	532	484	100	100

2015-16 average

Ireland	Current USD million	Constant 2017 USD mln	% share	Memo: DAC countries' average %
Ethiopia	39	40	9	
Mozambique	36	36	8	
Tanzania	30	30	7	
Uganda	26	26	6	
Malawi	22	22	5	
Top 5 recipients	152	155	36	21
Zambia	16	16	4	
Viet Nam	12	12	3	
Sierra Leone	12	12	3	
South Sudan	11	11	3	
Syrian Arab Republic	10	10	2	
Top 10 recipients	213	217	50	33
Kenya	8	8	2	
Somalia	7	7	2	
Zimbabwe	7	7	2	
Democratic Republic of the Congo	6	6	1	
South Africa	6	6	1	
Top 15 recipients	248	252	58	41
Central African Republic	6	6	1	
West Bank and Gaza Strip	6	6	1	
Sudan	6	6	1	
Liberia	3	3	1	
Turkey				
Top 20 recipients	275	280	64	47
Total (140 recipients)	323	329	76	
Unallocated	104	106	24	41
Total bilateral gross	427	435	100	100

2017-18 average

Ireland	Current USD million	Constant 2017 USD mln	% share	Memo: DAC countries' average % [1]
Ethiopia	42	41	8	
Uganda	30	29	6	
Mozambique	27	26	5	
Tanzania	26	25	5	
Malawi	24	23	5	
Top 5 recipients	148	145	29	18
Sierra Leone	14	14	3	
South Sudan	13	12	2	
Turkey	11	10	2	
Zambia	10	10	2	
Viet Nam	10	10	2	
Top 10 recipients	206	201	40	30
Democratic Republic of the Congo	10	10	2	
Zimbabwe	8	8	2	
Kenya	8	7	1	
Central African Republic	7	7	1	
Somalia	7	7	1	
Top 15 recipients	247	241	48	37
Sudan	7	6	1	
West Bank and Gaza Strip	6	6	1	
Syrian Arab Republic	6	6	1	
Yemen	6	6	1	
Lebanon	5	5		
Top 20 recipients	277	270	54	42
Total (142 recipients)	333	325	65	
Unallocated	179	174	35	54
Total bilateral gross	512	499	100	100

Gross disbursements

Note: (1) 2017 data.

StatLink https://doi.org/10.1787/888934121335

Table B.5. Bilateral ODA by major purposes

Commitments - Two-year average

Ireland	2013-14 average		2015-16 average		2017-18 average		DAC
	2017 USD million	%	2017 USD million	%	2017 USD million	%	2017 %
Social infrastructure & services	**234**	**51**	**202**	**49**	**209**	**45**	**34**
Education	43	9	37	9	39	8	7
of which: basic education	10	2	10	2	16	3	2
Health	76	16	58	14	60	13	5
of which: basic health	39	8	28	7	32	7	3
Population & reproductive health	12	3	12	3	9	2	6
Water supply & sanitation	5	1	6	2	6	1	4
Government & civil society	73	16	64	16	69	15	10
of which: Conflict, peace & security	8	2	9	2	10	2	3
Other social infrastructure & services	25	5	23	6	26	6	2
Economic infrastructure & services	**4**	**1**	**3**	**1**	**3**	**1**	**17**
Transport & storage	-	-	0	0	0	0	8
Communications	0	0	0	0	0	0	0
Energy	0	0	0	0	0	0	6
Banking & financial services	0	0	0	0	1	0	2
Business & other services	3	1	3	1	2	0	1
Production sectors	**44**	**9**	**33**	**8**	**36**	**8**	**7**
Agriculture, forestry & fishing	42	9	32	8	33	7	5
Industry, mining & construction	0	0	1	0	1	0	1
Trade & tourism	1	0	1	0	1	0	1
Multisector	**22**	**5**	**20**	**5**	**27**	**6**	**8**
Commodity and programme aid	**35**	**8**	**18**	**4**	**2**	**0**	**3**
Action relating to debt	**-**	**-**	**0**	**0**	**-**	**-**	**0**
Humanitarian aid	**92**	**20**	**103**	**25**	**113**	**24**	**13**
Administrative costs of donors	**31**	**7**	**31**	**8**	**31**	**7**	**6**
Refugees in donor countries	**0**	**0**	**1**	**0**	**47**	**10**	**11**
Total bilateral allocable	**460**	**100**	**411**	**100**	**467**	**100**	**100**
For reference:							
Total bilateral	484	64	435	56	499	58	76
of which: Unallocated	23	3	24	3	32	4	0
Total multilateral	271	36	339	44	365	42	24
Total ODA	**755**	**100**	**774**	**100**	**864**	**100**	**100**

Commitments

	2013-14		2015-16		2017-18	
	Constant 2017 USD million	% Bilateral allocable	Constant 2017 USD million	% Bilateral allocable	Constant 2017 USD million	% Bilateral allocable
Gender equality	198	46	307	78	331	80
Environment	71	16	84	22	95	23
Rio markers						
Biodiversity	35	8	35	9	50	12
Desertification	31	7	31	8	48	12
Climate change, mitigation only	3	1	0	0	1	0
Climate change, adaptation only	27	6	37	9	33	8
Both climate adaptation and mitigation	42	10	41	10	59	14

StatLink ᴍᴸ https://doi.org/10.1787/888934121354

Table B.6. Comparative aid performance of DAC members

	Official development assistance			Net disbursements				Commitments	
	2017		2011-12 to 2016-17 Average annual % change in real terms	Share of multilateral aid 2017				Grant element of ODA commitments 2017	Untied aid % of bilateral commitments 2017
				% of ODA		% of GNI			
	USD million	% of GNI		(b)	(c)	(b)	(c)	% (a)	(d)
Australia	3 036	0.23	-4.2	20.5		0.05		100.0	100.0
Austria	1 251	0.30	7.4	52.0	25.2	0.16	0.08	100.0	50.1
Belgium	2 196	0.45	-0.2	41.0	12.2	0.18	0.05	99.9	95.6
Canada	4 305	0.26	-1.5	27.4		0.07		94.5	93.9
Czech Republic	304	0.15	7.4	73.5	17.1	0.11	0.03	100.0	55.9
Denmark	2 448	0.74	-0.5	29.7	18.2	0.22	0.13	100.0	100.0
Finland	1 084	0.42	-2.9	44.8	21.8	0.19	0.09	100.0	98.3
France	11 331	0.43	-0.7	41.3	20.1	0.18	0.09	81.0	96.1
Germany	25 005	0.67	15.2	20.7	8.8	0.14	0.06	90.2	85.5
Greece	314	0.16	2.7	73.0	12.0	0.11	0.02	100.0	90.6
Hungary	149	0.11	9.4	73.5	16.5	0.08	0.02	100.0	..
Iceland	68	0.28	14.7	20.7		0.06		100.0	100.0
Ireland	838	0.32	0.9	41.2	17.0	0.13	0.05	100.0	100.0
Italy	5 858	0.30	12.2	49.2	19.1	0.15	0.06	98.8	90.9
Japan	11 463	0.23	6.2	29.5		0.07		85.4	82.5
Korea	2 201	0.14	7.7	26.6		0.04		93.2	50.2
Luxembourg	424	1.00	2.3	28.3	19.5	0.28	0.19	100.0	98.8
Netherlands	4 958	0.60	-0.7	28.7	16.9	0.17	0.10	100.0	94.9
New Zealand	450	0.23	1.3	17.6		0.04		100.0	74.6
Norway	4 125	0.99	5.0	24.2		0.24		100.0	100.0
Poland	679	0.13	13.8	67.3	9.5	0.09	0.01	99.6	60.3
Portugal	381	0.18	-8.9	69.9	21.7	0.13	0.04	97.2	68.6
Slovak Republic	119	0.13	10.0	70.3	8.5	0.09	0.01	100.0	62.2
Slovenia	76	0.16	8.1	67.1	11.9	0.11	0.02	100.0	99.6
Spain	2 560	0.19	5.5	73.3	27.8	0.14	0.05	99.1	83.5
Sweden	5 563	1.02	2.8	31.2	23.9	0.32	0.24	100.0	89.7
Switzerland	3 138	0.46	4.0	25.7		0.12		100.0	96.5
United Kingdom	18 103	0.70	7.8	37.4	27.8	0.26	0.19	95.5	100.0
United States	34 732	0.18	0.8	13.6		0.02		100.0	63.5
Total DAC	**147 160**	**0.31**	**4.3**	**28.3**		**0.09**		**93.6**	**82.0**

Notes:
a. Excluding debt reorganisation.
b. Including EU institutions.
c. Excluding EU institutions.
d. Excluding administrative costs and in-donor refugee costs.
.. Data not available.

StatLink https://doi.org/10.1787/888934121373

Table B.7. Comparative performance of aid to LDCs

	Bilateral ODA to LDCs			Total ODA to LDCs (Bilateral and through multilateral agencies) 2017			Grant element of bilateral ODA commitments[a] to LDCs (two alternative norms)		
	2017	2017					Annually for all LDCs Norm: 90%		3-year average for each LDC Norm: 86%
	USD million	% bilateral ODA	% of GNI	USD million	% total ODA	% of GNI	2016	2017	2015-2017
Australia	665	27.6	0.05	852	28.1	0.07	100.0	100.0	c
Austria	63	10.5	0.02	293	23.4	0.07	100.0	100.0	c
Belgium	402	31.0	0.08	649	29.6	0.13	99.3	99.8	c
Canada	957	30.6	0.06	1 486	34.5	0.09	100.0	100.0	c
Czech Republic	13	15.8	0.01	64	21.1	0.03	100.0	100.0	c
Denmark	472	27.4	0.14	729	29.8	0.22	100.0	100.0	c
Finland	166	27.7	0.06	325	30.0	0.13	100.0	100.0	c
France	1 129	17.0	0.04	2 753	24.3	0.10	80.8	75.1	n
Germany	2 423	12.2	0.06	4 089	16.4	0.11	95.9	99.8	n
Greece	0	0.2	0.00	56	18.0	0.03	100.0	100.0	c
Hungary	4	11.0	0.00	29	19.2	0.02	100.0	100.0	c
Iceland	14	25.4	0.06	20	28.6	0.08	100.0	100.0	c
Ireland	248	50.4	0.09	359	42.9	0.14	100.0	100.0	c
Italy	326	11.0	0.02	1 161	19.8	0.06	98.8	97.5	c
Japan	3 358	41.6	0.07	5 001	43.6	0.10	91.5	87.8	n
Korea	588	36.4	0.04	780	35.4	0.05	93.0	94.6	c
Luxembourg	141	46.4	0.33	182	42.9	0.43	100.0	100.0	c
Netherlands	546	15.5	0.07	1 045	21.1	0.13	100.0	100.0	c
New Zealand	102	27.6	0.05	127	28.3	0.07	100.0	100.0	c
Norway	733	23.4	0.18	1 165	28.2	0.28	100.0	100.0	c
Poland	14	6.4	0.00	113	16.6	0.02	80.4	85.0	n
Portugal	43	37.7	0.02	123	32.4	0.06	92.2	94.4	n
Slovak Republic	4	9.9	0.00	22	18.7	0.02	100.0	100.0	c
Slovenia	0	1.8	0.00	12	16.3	0.03	100.0	100.0	c
Spain	97	14.2	0.01	584	22.8	0.04	100.0	100.0	c
Sweden	1 023	26.7	0.19	1 708	30.7	0.31	100.0	100.0	c
Switzerland	574	24.6	0.08	922	29.4	0.13	100.0	100.0	c
United Kingdom	3 319	29.3	0.13	6 081	33.6	0.23	100.0	100.0	c
United States	10 008	33.4	0.05	12 091	34.8	0.06	100.0	100.0	c
Total DAC	**27 433**	**26.0**	**0.06**	**42 823**	**29.1**	**0.09**	**100.0**	**100.0**	..

Notes:
a. Excluding debt reorganisation. Equities are treated as having 100% grant element, but are not treated as loans.
b. c = compliance, n = non compliance.
.. Data not available.

StatLink https://doi.org/10.1787/888934121392

Figure B.1. Net ODA from DAC countries in 2018

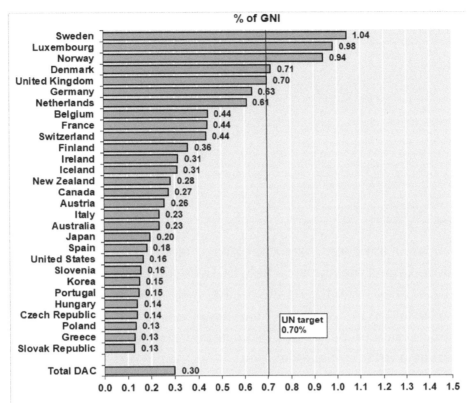

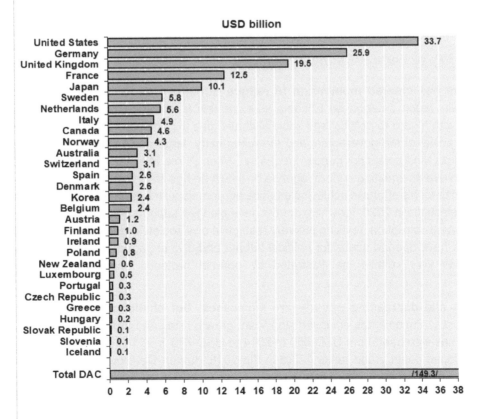

StatLink 🖼️ https://doi.org/10.1787/888934121221

Annex C. Field visit to Ethiopia

As part of the peer review of Ireland, a team of reviewers from Australia and Slovenia and members of the OECD Secretariat visited Ethiopia in October 2019. They met the team of the Irish embassy in Ethiopia, the Irish ambassador to Tanzania, representatives of national authorities, bilateral and multilateral partners, Ethiopian and Irish civil society organisations, the private sector, and researchers.

Development in Ethiopia

Impressive progress and daunting challenges

Political reform has created momentum to reduce Ethiopia's extreme fragility. The 2018 OECD *States of Fragility* report categorised Ethiopia as extremely fragile (OECD, 2018[1]). The country faces severe fragility with regard to political and societal challenges in particular. This relates to factors such as the unchecked power of the government and the ruling party, large-scale internal displacement resulting from local conflicts, and persistent gender inequality. When Prime Minister Abiy Ahmed Ali took office in 2018, he put forward an ambitious reform agenda on which he has started to deliver. He received the 2019 Nobel Peace Prize for his efforts in achieving a peace agreement with Eritrea. At home, Abiy has committed to free and fair elections in 2020, for which donors have pledged support. Allowing political parties to work, fighting government corruption, revising the very restrictive civil society organisation (CSO) legislation and other measures have opened space for political debate and civil engagement. However, the situation in Ethiopia remains very volatile, as illustrated by political protests, ongoing violence and massive displacement.

Strong growth and decreasing poverty are successes, but challenges loom large. While still a low-income country, Ethiopia has achieved significant growth rates and gross national income per capita (Atlas method) has increased from USD 550 in 2014 to USD 790 in 2018 (World Bank, 2019[2]). Ethiopia is a least developed country and ranks 173rd in the 2018 Human Development Index (UNDP, 2019[3]). Absolute poverty dropped from 33.5% in 2010 to 30.5% in 2015 (USD 1.9 per day 2011 purchasing power parity), and living standards improved. Foreign direct investment (FDI) declined by 18% from 2017 to 2018, to USD 3.3 billion, but the country is still the biggest recipient of FDI in East Africa and accounts for more than one third of all FDI reaching the sub-region (UNCTAD, 2019[4]). At the same time, the share of tax revenue in Ethiopia's gross domestic product remains among the lowest in Africa (World Bank, 2019[2]).

The International Monetary Fund warns of a high risk of debt distress and recommends restraint on non-concessional loans while protecting pro-poor spending programmes (International Monetary Fund, 2018[5]). Agriculture remains by far the dominant economic sector, employing 80% of the population, and this makes Ethiopia highly vulnerable to natural hazards such as drought that climate change is expected to exacerbate. Population growth is still very high. The population of an estimated 109 million in 2018 is anticipated to grow to more than 205 million by 2050, putting pressure on services and job markets (UN, 2019[61]).

Ethiopia aims to become a lower middle-income country by 2025 by focusing on economic growth as well as pro-poor policies. Consistent with the overall aim to reduce poverty, the country's second Growth and Transformation Plan 2016-2020 sets a target of average annual growth of 11% through greater productivity and competitiveness (Ethiopia National Planning Commission, 2015[6]). The government intends to advance critical reforms in this area while also seeking support from donors, which are organised in the Development Assistance Group (DAG). Public service reform, investment in human development, and women and youth empowerment are other priorities under the Growth and Transformation Plan. The social protection, flagship programme, Productive Safety Net Programme, illustrates the government's pro-poor approach.

Figure C.1. Aid at a glance, Ethiopia

Receipts	2015	2016	2017
Net ODA (USD million)	3 235	4 074	4 117
Bilateral share (gross ODA)	57%	50%	53%
Net ODA / GNI	5.0%	5.6%	5.1%
Other Official Flows (USD million)	226	156	786
Net Private flows (USD million)	656	705	352
Total net receipts (USD million)	4 118	4 934	5 255

For reference	2015	2016	2017
Population (million)	99.9	102.4	105.0
GNI per capita (Atlas USD)	600	660	740

Top Ten Donors of gross ODA (2016-17 average)	(USD m)
1 International Development Association	1 154
2 United States	954
3 United Kingdom	437
4 EU Institutions	279
5 African Development Fund	209
6 Global Fund	170
7 Germany	148
8 Canada	90
9 Netherlands	78
10 Global Alliance for Vaccines and Immunization	74

Bilateral ODA by Sector (2016-17)

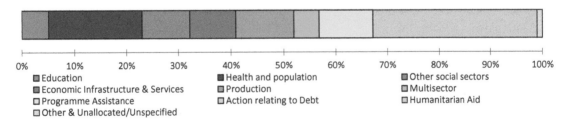

■ Education
■ Economic Infrastructure & Services
☐ Programme Assistance
☐ Other & Unallocated/Unspecified
■ Health and population
☐ Production
☐ Action relating to Debt
☐ Other social sectors
☐ Multisector
☐ Humanitarian Aid

Source: OECD (2020[7]), Aid at a glance (webpage), http://www.oecd.org/dac/financing-sustainable-development/development-finance-data/aid-at-a-glance.htm.

StatLink 🔗 https://doi.org/10.1787/888934121240

Towards a comprehensive Irish development effort

Development co-operation is at the centre of Ireland's engagement with Ethiopia

Since the opening of the Irish Embassy in Ethiopia in 1994, development co-operation has continued to be the defining feature of Irish-Ethiopian relations. Ethiopia is Ireland's largest aid recipient, receiving an average USD 41 million per year from 2014-17. This represents 12% of total Irish allocated ODA over this period. Officials from Ireland have made numerous high-level visits to Ethiopia over the past few years through which Ireland has aimed to expand the scope of relations including by signing a double taxation agreement and initiating private sector initiatives. However, trade between the countries is minimal, with exports to Ethiopia amounting to USD 38 million and imports from Ethiopia of USD 5 million in 2017 (World Integrated Trade Solution, 2019[8]). A handful of Irish companies operate in Ethiopia, and a few citizens from each country live in the other. The Irish Ambassador in Addis Ababa is also accredited to regional organisations,[1] South Sudan and Djibouti. While Ireland will reflect all these aspects in its forthcoming whole-of-mission strategy, the primary focus will continue to be its development co-operation.

Ireland's foreign policy priorities are reflected in its political engagement in Ethiopia. For many years and in a challenging political context, Ireland has been exercising leadership in promoting civic space, mobilising the donor community and engaging with the government. Ireland also remains a strong advocate for gender equality and against gender-based violence. Ireland intends to strengthen the focus on gender equality under the new country strategy, whereby greater donor leadership could add value in a challenging environment. Ireland's principled political engagement on internal displacement has helped to drive acknowledgement of the challenge and garner support for a response. The government and partners appreciated Ireland's efforts to promote a humanitarian-development nexus through social protection.

Policy coherence is not part of monitoring or dialogue. Where Ireland's policies relate to collective global action, they can indirectly affect Ethiopia's development. While Ireland will miss its greenhouse gas emission targets and only in 2019 adopted a more ambitious plan for climate action, Ethiopia is significantly exposed to risks of climate change, takes adaptive action and undertook a massive tree planting project to help to mitigate emissions. Ethiopia also hosts a large number of refugees. The Irish Embassy in Ethiopia does not report back to Dublin on potential challenges to policy coherence, although Ethiopia has not raised any such issues with Ireland as either an individual state or as member state of the European Union (EU). Nevertheless, adding this dimension to political dialogue could enhance Ireland's voice in discussions at both global and country level.

Ireland's policies, strategies and ODA allocation

The new mission strategy is an opportunity for Ireland to deliver on the priorities of A Better World

The new mission strategy is an opportunity for Ireland to focus its efforts. The previous 2015-18 strategy, now extended to 2019, matched up Ethiopian challenges and Irish priorities well as it focused on work in agriculture, social protection, health, nutrition and civil society. However, Ireland's development assistance to Ethiopia corresponds to only 1% of official development assistance (ODA) to Ethiopia in 2017.[2] In the same year, Ireland is the 18th largest of all donors in Ethiopia recorded in OECD development co-operation statistics. Even in its concentration sectors, Irish ODA represents only about 2% of total donor disbursements in the country. Partners thus felt there was potential for a deepened, rather than a broadened, Irish engagement. In addition, the growth of Ireland's portfolio in terms of output areas and number of partnerships in Ethiopia put the Embassy's capacities under strain. In response, the Embassy intends to sharpen the focus of its programme under the new country strategy. Initial planning under the next country strategy foresees a static budget, which could be increased after a mid-term review as Ireland plans to increase ODA. In order to preserve quality and focus over time, such plans would need to anticipate where Ireland could increase spending and the staffing capacity this would require.

Policy guidance from headquarters could make a significant difference in translating the priorities of *A Better World* in Ethiopia. The Embassy invests heavily in internal reflections for the development of its new country strategy (as elaborated further in this section). Anticipated choices indicate continuity in areas of previous focus, social protection and civil society space, and continuing climate change as a cross-cutting issue. *A Better World* pushed the Embassy to develop new priorities focusing on gender equality and strengthening governance in public institutions. More policy guidance from the DFAT headquarters in Ireland could help the Embassy to ensure a programme that is focused on Irish policy priorities while responding to shifting expectations and opportunities in Ethiopia. For instance, a specific focus on furthest behind first will raise challenging questions of targeting, approach and trade-offs in terms of time horizon, results and risks. The Department of Foreign Affairs and Trade (DFAT) has indicted that Ireland would like to concentrate on areas where its four policy priorities intersect.[3] Such a focus could allow Ireland to use its limited human resources to maximum effect by deepening expertise in clearly identified areas.

The preparation of mission strategies now involves the identification of a broad theory of change, within which Ireland's added value is taken into account and a number of outcomes and associated results are identified. Sectors and programmes in which Ireland has been previously engaged play a significant role in the decision-making process, and the five-year budget plans for mission strategies reflect historic levels of allocations as well as the embassy's absorption capacity. However, missions are now in the position to make more strategic choices around engaging in new sectors or changing the way they are engaging in current sectors. In the past, previous mission strategies were more prescriptive and could reference specific partners, limiting adaptability during the strategy period.

Programmes financed by headquarters are not part of the Ethiopia country strategy. These include both programmes financed by DFAT, notably its Humanitarian Unit and the Civil Society and Development Education Unit, and by other departments, such as the technical co-operation provided by the Health Service Executive. The Embassy in Ethiopia is aware of these programmes and there is consultation between DFAT in Dublin and Ireland's embassies on planned interventions. The new country strategy could identify ways to better reflect all Irish bilateral and multilateral contributions, including those from other departments.

Ireland's private sector engagement in Ethiopia could provide useful lessons for focusing its efforts in other partner countries and globally. The ambitious Ethiopian economic reform agenda coupled with a challenging local business environment provide for great opportunities but also risks for private sector engagement through development co-operation. While many larger players are active in Ethiopia, private sector counterparts appreciate the advice, advocacy and matchmaking efforts of the Embassy of Ireland, which often add greater value than Ireland's limited financial engagement.[4] This can be particularly effective when done in concert with other donors, including those that provide significant financial support to help to improve Ethiopia's business environment. Ireland's private sector engagement in Ethiopia can also contribute insights on how private sector activities can help to improve the lives of marginalised populations, especially in the agri-food and IT sector. As Ireland is developing its new strategy for its private sector engagement on a global scale, it could ultimately draw on the experience it gains from such engagement in Ethiopia.

It is not yet clear how Ireland's regional engagement, which is very limited in scale, will add value. Through its diplomatic mission in Ethiopia, Ireland has started to co-operate with regional institutions; the Embassy in Tanzania also includes countries of secondary accreditation in its mission strategy, in line with Ireland's ambition to increase its global footprint. Since 2018, Ireland deployed a policy officer to Addis

116 |

Ababa as deputy representative to the AU, to liaise with the African Union and the Inter-Governmental Authority on Development. This provides Ireland with access to institutions and intelligence that can inform decision making. However, in this initial phase, co-operation programmes with these institutions are very small.[5] If Ireland chooses to pursue a dedicated regional engagement, it would benefit from defining what its contribution to regional development could be, how a regional approach would complement and link with its bilateral engagement, and which resources it needs to mobilise for this.

Figure C.2. Ireland's ODA to Ethiopia by sector

Commitments, millions USD, 2017 constant prices

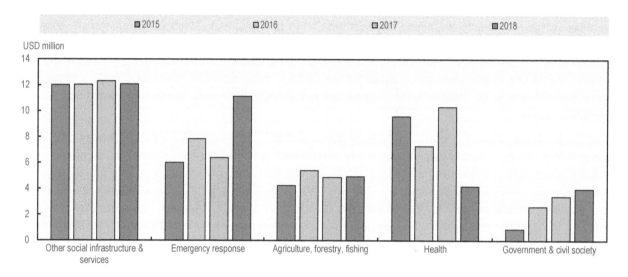

Source: Based on data from (OECD, 2019[9]), *Creditor Reporting System* (database), https://stats.oecd.org/Index.aspx?DataSetCode=crs1 (accessed January 2020).

StatLink https://doi.org/10.1787/888934121259

Organisation and management

Empowered embassy staff are an asset to Ireland's engagement

Ireland's embassies have clear and sufficient authority. Embassies are responsible for designing country strategies, which are then approved by DFAT senior management. Like units in DFAT headquarters in Ireland, these have authority to make commitments and disbursements for projects with a value of up to EUR 1.5 million per year, unless risks or relevance require approval at a higher level. In practice, most financial engagements fall within this limit and only larger contributions to multi-donor programmes exceed the ceiling, although this might change if the aid budget grows substantially. Embassies thus have a significant level of autonomy regarding programmatic decisions. DFAT headquarters is responsible for decisions on the creation of posts, while embassies manage recruitment. This sometimes delays the replacement of existing positions.

Collaboration between DFAT headquarters and missions generally works well. DFAT headquarters systematically consults embassies on the development of policies and guidance. Despite capacity constraints, the headquarters also manages to give approval or provide advice in a timely and substantive manner. DFAT headquarters representatives also participated in workshops for the design of the new Ethiopia country strategy. Additionally, a new e-submission system makes the work stream for submissions to management more transparent for embassies.

Local staff are critical to the implementation of Ireland's bilateral co-operation. In Ethiopia, the head of development and two deputies are filled by Irish personnel posted to Ethiopia. The 11 sector and programme leads are locally hired staff. Local staff manage grants, inform political dialogue, bring technical expertise and local knowledge, and hold institutional memory. They are empowered to represent Ireland in policy discussions, and partners value their quality engagement. Ireland invests in their skills development so local staff can profit from training opportunities (including abroad) identified through the annual performance management review. As opportunities for career progression within the Irish Embassy are limited, some staff have chosen to pursue their careers elsewhere. However, retention of staff is strongly aided by the overall satisfaction of personnel with working conditions. Within the Embassy, local staff are highly valued and integrated. Their contracts apply the more beneficial clauses of either Irish or Ethiopian law. The Embassy compensates overtime work, salaries are increased regularly and DFAT headquarters has approved additional human resources to address a growing workload. The Embassy solicited and reflected comments by local staff in the staff manual, which is available in Amharic. A service desk at HQ for local staff exists, but local staff representatives are not consulted by HQ on human resources policies.

The Embassy's efforts on risk management are strong and it is committed to learning

The Embassy plays an important role in risk management. Staff systematically work to ensure that financial, operational and other risks are appropriately assessed and that safeguards are in place. Management and staff regularly discuss and update the risk register. The Embassy takes a range of mitigating measures where necessary, ranging from capacity building to adjusting intervention approaches or suspending payments. As the system strongly relies on the assessment and diligence of individual staff, forthcoming guidance on safeguarding could provide them the assurance that they have fulfilled all necessary minimum standards of risk management. A timely update of the country corruption profile will be important to inform the country strategy. It will also be an opportunity to discuss how the Embassy can institutionalise work on anti-corruption, including through training on anti-corruption awareness. Guidance on the handling of cases of suspected fraud could also be useful, in particular to clarify what constitutes a suspected case of fraud, notably in relation to audit findings.

The Embassy shows a strong commitment to learning but cannot fully seize opportunities for documenting and sharing lessons. In the design of its new mission strategy, the Embassy has invested significantly in internal reflection, drawing on the evaluation of the previous country strategy, external analysis and contributions from Embassy staff across all services. Grant managers encourage programme adaptations in response to monitoring findings and, on occasion, share their technical expertise with other Irish missions. However, the Embassy does not document knowledge in a way that could contribute to broader institutional learning, due to systemic constraints. The e-grant management system that is currently piloted would be an opportunity to enable the capturing of knowledge locally and ensuring it is accessible both at headquarters and other missions. Together with further investments in information technology infrastructure, this system could also facilitate data management.

Partnerships, results and accountability

Ireland is a much-appreciated partner to the Ethiopian government, donors and CSOs

Ireland is an active and energetic donor, taking a proactive role in political dialogue and donor co-ordination. As a key member of the DAG, Ireland is seen as a driver of open, informed dialogue that puts the interests of Ethiopia first. It is also regarded as an honest broker among development partners and with the Ethiopian government and other stakeholders. Ireland is actively involved, as member of the DAG Executive Committee, co-chair of both the Humanitarian Resilience Donor Group and the Donor Working Group of the Productive Safety Net Programme and lead in the Civil Society Support Programme.

Ireland smartly uses these opportunities to act as strategic influencer despite its limited financial weight. As EU donor co-ordination does not offer the same opportunities of member state leadership, Ireland finds itself in a competitive environment in Ethiopia, where 20 other EU member states are active. Continuing to focus on a limited set of priorities that link to its own portfolio, partnering with like-minded donors, and strategically engaging Irish and local CSOs are likely Ireland's best avenues to add value within the overall contributions of EU donors.

In its partnership with the Ethiopian government, Ireland delivers high-quality development co-operation with some scope for improvement. Ireland aligns to national priorities, provides aid on budget, and uses country public financial management systems where possible and appropriate. It is transparent, providing timely, comprehensive and reliable information through the Ethiopian Aid Management Platform. While it ensures good annual predictability, Ireland could improve provision of forward-looking expenditure plans to the Ethiopian government, building on the five-year budget planning that underpins the country strategy. The Irish Embassy holds regular dialogue with line ministries at sectoral and programmatic level to inform decision making and establish mutual accountability. In contrast, Ireland had not yet involved the government in early-stage strategic discussions on the next country strategy, also due to evolving policy shifts on both sides. In the same vein, only two of five priorities and/or outputs of the 2014-19 country strategy were jointly agreed with Ethiopia (OECD/UNDP, 2019[10]). Ethiopia was informed about progress in implementing the strategy but was not part of joint evaluations. Late consultation with the government risks that the best match may not be found between Ireland's offer and Ethiopia's development priorities.

Ireland is widely appreciated as a committed and reliable development partner in Ethiopia, in particular among CSOs. It provides focused support, often channelled through multi-donor pooled funds, that gives implementing partners the flexibility in their programming to adapt to changing contexts. Ireland engages in multi-annual agreements with a range of partners in Ethiopia. In some cases, year-by-year disbursements impede predictability and planning. By providing funding in areas where needs are greatest, Ireland is considered an indispensable partner for CSOs. Dialogue and learning opportunities between the Embassy and Irish and local CSOs abound. More formalised dialogue could make information sharing between the Embassy and CSO partners more efficient.

More policy guidance from DFAT headquarters on selecting channels and modalities could inform decision making at mission level. In line with its support of national ownership, the Embassy has expressed a commitment to partner with the Ethiopian government where possible and Irish assistance in Ethiopia already is implemented mainly through the channel of the public sector. At the same time, Ireland values its partnerships with both CSOs and multilaterals, and seeks to engage more strongly with the private sector. The Embassy has not had guidance from DFAT headquarters in the preparation of the new country strategy regarding the matching of Ireland's objectives and possible channels. When it selects partners within a specific channel, Ireland proceeds by direct awards of its project-level grants. It sometimes explores a range of suitable partners, in particular for new initiatives, there is requirement to document if alternative partners were considered, and if not, why not. This might have drawbacks in terms of lower value for money if partners feel that funding is likely regardless of value added or strong performance.

Ireland has been able to significantly adapt to changes in the overall context and aid programmes

A good understanding of the domestic context informs Ireland's actions and good responsiveness. Ireland stands out as a quick responder to changing political and humanitarian contexts, for example by reacting swiftly to recent climate and conflict shocks in 2016 and 2018. For the design of its new country strategy, the Embassy complemented its political intelligence with a meta-analysis on poverty, vulnerability and inequality and drew on existing analysis by other donors. It also conducted political economy analyses for its civil society and social protection engagement and shared these with other donors. In an effort to accompany political reform, it is supporting the next elections and is the first donor to have entered a new partnership with the Ethiopian parliament. Basing Embassy staff in Ethiopian regions gives Ireland a good understanding of local realities. This is particularly important in a context where regional governments are assuming increasing responsibility. Ireland also promotes innovative approaches. It has supported pilots on e-payments and nutrition-sensitive social protection that generated evidence to inform discussions with the Ethiopian government and donors for potential scale-up.

Ireland regularly monitors results and uses them to adapt its programme design and implementation. Grant managers assess progress reports, make regular monitoring visits, document their findings and discuss with implementing partners how to adjust course. Although sometimes asked by HQ colleagues, the Embassy is not expected to and does not have the capacity to monitor implementation of HQ financed programmes. Specific staff capacity could help to ensure the quality of monitoring frameworks on aspects such as ambition, data availability and alignment with Ethiopian frameworks and could also provide advice on the design of locally commissioned evaluations. The update of Ethiopia's development strategy presents an opportunity for the Embassy, with headquarters support, to align the new country strategy results framework to both Ethiopia's own performance monitoring and its own forthcoming accountability and results framework under *A Better World*.

References

Ethiopia National Planning Commission (2015), *Growth and Transformation Plan II*, https://ethiopia.un.org/sites/default/files/2019-08/GTPII%20%20English%20Translation%20%20Final%20%20June%2021%202016.pdf. [6]

International Monetary Fund (2018), *IMF Country Report: The Federal Democratic Republic of Ethiopia*, https://www.imf.org/~/media/Files/Publications/CR/2018/cr18354.ashx. [5]

OECD (2020), *Aid at a glance (Webpage)*, http://www.oecd.org/dac/financing-sustainable-development/development-finance-data/aid-at-a-glance.htm. [7]

OECD (2019), *Creditor Reporting System (database)*, https://stats.oecd.org/Index.aspx?DataSetCode=crs1. [9]

OECD (2018), *States of Fragility 2018*, OECD Publishing, Paris, https://dx.doi.org/10.1787/9789264302075-en. [1]

OECD/UNDP (2019), *Making Development Co-operation More Effective: 2019 Progress Report*, OECD Publishing, Paris, https://doi.org/10.1787/26f2638f-en. [10]

UNCTAD (2019), *World Investment Report 2019: Special Economic Zones*, United Nations Conference on Trade and Development (UNCTAD), Geneva, https://unctad.org/en/PublicationsLibrary/wir2019_en.pdf. [4]

UNDP (2019), *2019 Human Development Index Ranking*, http://hdr.undp.org/en/content/2019-human-development-index-ranking (accessed on 12 December 2019). [3]

World Bank (2019), *World Development Indicators (database)*, https://databank.worldbank.org/data/reports.aspx?source=world-development-indicators (accessed on 25 April 2019). [2]

World Integrated Trade Solution (2019), *WITS - Ethiopia (excludes Eritrea) trade statistics (database)*, World Integrated Trade Solution, https://wits.worldbank.org/CountryProfile/en/ETH (accessed on 25 April 2019).

[8]

Notes

[1] The Embassy also covers the African Union, the Inter-Governmental Authority on Development and the UN Economic Commission for Africa.

[2] Figures from 2017 (OECD, 2019[9]). In this sense, Ethiopia is representative of most of Ireland's priority countries in that it is a large ODA recipient with numerous active donors.

[3] This would prioritise gender equality, strengthening of governance, reduction of humanitarian need and climate change.

[4] Irish private sector partnerships in Ethiopia include the electronic payment system, including to social safety net beneficiaries, provided by the Irish company M-Birr; Irish Aid partially financed the start-up phase and the European Investment Bank invested significantly in M-Birr. Another partnership involves AfricaJuice, a Dutch-Irish enterprise that produces and exports tropical fruit juices from Ethiopia and employs over 2 000 people. In addition, Moyee Coffee sources coffee in Ethiopia.

[5] Ireland's support to the African Union amounts to EUR 300 000. As a comparison, donor support to the organisation totals to about 1 000 times this amount per year.

Annex D. Organisational charts

Figure D.1. Organisation of the Irish Foreign Service

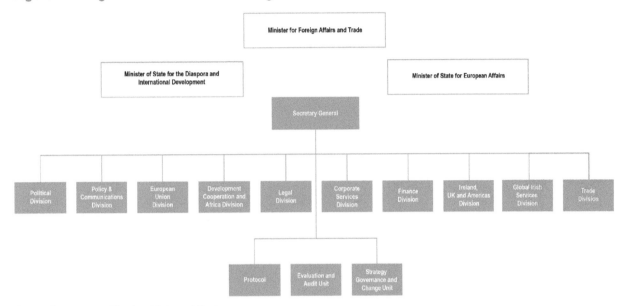

Source: Department of Foreign Affairs and Trade.

Figure D.2. Organisational structure of the DFAT Development Cooperation and Africa Division

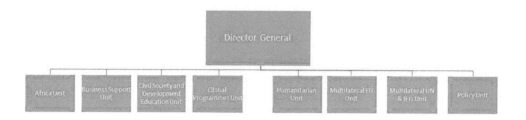

Source: Department of Foreign Affairs and Trade.

Lightning Source UK Ltd.
Milton Keynes UK
UKHW050752010620
364110UK00002B/5